# Commanding God
# or
# Making Up God's Mind

## Using the Higher Power That Works In, Through and For You

### Jon William Lopez, LSP

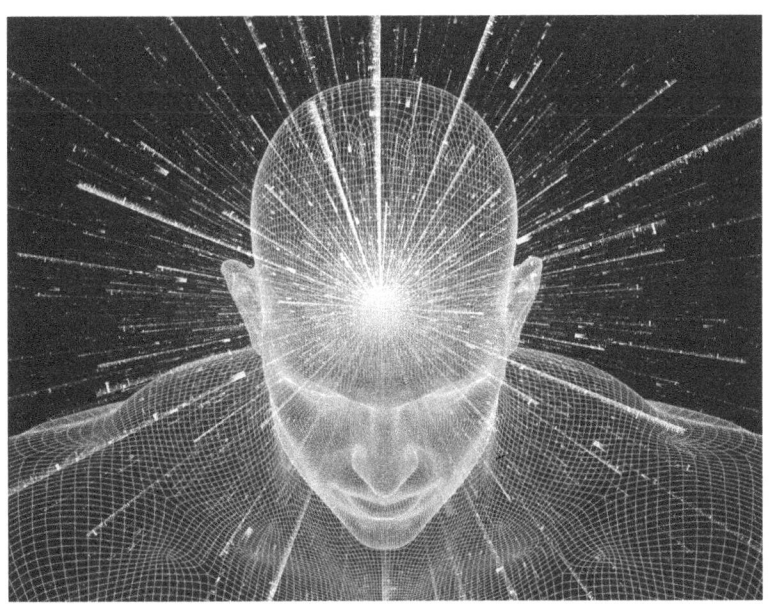

CCB Publishing
British Columbia, Canada

Commanding God or Making Up God's Mind:
Using the Higher Power That Works In, Through and For You

Copyright ©2023 by Jon William Lopez, LSP
ISBN-13   978-1-77143-555-0
First Edition

Library and Archives Canada Cataloguing in Publication
Title: Commanding God or making up God's mind: using the higher power that works in, through and for you / by Jon William Lopez, LSP.
Names: Lopez, Jon William, 1952-, author.
Description: First edition.
Identifiers: Canadiana (print) 20230142486 | Canadiana (ebook) 20230143202 | ISBN 9781771435550 (softcover) | ISBN 9781771435567 (PDF)
Subjects: LCSH: Self-actualization (Psychology)—Religious aspects—Christianity. | LCSH: God—Will. | LCSH: God—Omnipresence.
Classification: LCC BV4598.2 .L67 2023 | DDC 248.4—dc23

All graphic images contained herein including cover images are either used with permission, are in the Public Domain, have been licensed for use, or are the author's own work.

Photo of author is copyright by Jon William Lopez, LSP.

Extreme care has been taken by the author to ensure that all information presented in this book is accurate and up to date at the time of publishing. Neither the author nor the publisher can be held responsible for any errors or omissions. Additionally, neither is any liability assumed for damages resulting from the use of the information contained herein.

All rights reserved. No part of this publication may be reproduced, stored in a retrieval system or transmitted in any form or by any means, electronic, mechanical, photocopying, recording or otherwise without the express written permission of the author. If you would like to use material from the book, other than for review purposes, prior written permission must be obtained by contacting the author or publisher. Thank you for your support of the author's rights.

Publisher:    CCB Publishing
              British Columbia, Canada
              www.ccbpublishing.com

Dedicated to Tina, Coppelia, Zulma and Dagmar,
my cousins and spiritual siblings.

My spiritual sister Joan ("Sis")

My dear friends Leela and Keith Rama

Rev. Helen Street, who "sparked my spirit."

My soulmate and spouse Gray Povlin

Thank you all for saving my life on more than one occasion.
I never could have come this far without you.

# Preface

This book is the result of the learning, insight, spiritual growth and physical results (demonstrations) I have gained through my studies of the principles, concepts and ideas of New Thought spirituality, Thomas Troward (one of the founding fathers of the movement) and the teachings of the Science of Mind (Religious Science), one of the movement's major contemporary philosophies, founded by Dr. Ernest Holmes in 1916. The ideas and tools presented here, however, are universal and non-denominational and can be used by anyone of any belief system or religion. Spiritual laws, like the laws of physics, know nothing of any particular religion or dogma and hold true across the expanse of infinity, working whether we are aware of them or not. They work in varying degrees according to the breadth and strength of our belief, which is what sets them into motion. (And even if we don't "believe," the laws still work by appearing not to work!)

Throughout the book I occasionally use words, phrases, terminology and quotes from New Thought teachings and texts. In doing so, however, I in no way mean to infringe upon any copyrighted material, I only wish to better illustrate, clarify and strengthen a point or convey an idea that is universally true. The quotes in this book are used with permission.

# Contents

Preface ..................................................................... v

Introduction .............................................................. ix

Part 1 – A Mind Boggling Revelation ............................................ 1
    The Three Aspects of God ................................................. 5
    Your Concept of God ...................................................... 9
    Meditation-Visualization – My Concept of God ............................ 11

Part 2 – Commanding God Concepts ............................................ 17

Part 3 – Commanding God: Two Powerful and Effective Ways and Means for Making Up Its Mind ....................... 29

Part 4 – The Commanding God or "Goddammit" Treatment ....... 53

Part 5 – Post Prayer – Goddammit and Beyond ........................... 63

Part 6 – Further Techniques and Tools for "Using" God ............. 77

Part 7 – After Thoughts: Things to Keep in Consciousness When Commanding God ................................................. 85

Part 8 – Concluding Thoughts (And a Final "Revelation") .......... 97

A Brief History and Explanation of New Thought and the Science of Mind ................................................ 105

About the Author ..................................................... 109

Quotes and References .............................................. 111

Image Credits ........................................................ 113

*"From [an] individual point of view the universal creative power has no mind of its own, and therefore you can make up its mind for it."*

Thomas Troward
"The Edinburgh and Dore Lectures on Mental Science," 1909

Thomas Troward

# Introduction

There is a Higher Power in the Universe. In fact, this Power created the Universe. It is Intelligent and conscious.

Some call It God, Father or Lord. Some call It Spirit, Source, Higher Power, Divine Mind, Infinite Intelligence, or Cosmic Consciousness.

Whatever name you prefer to call It, It created you and all Life. It is not "out there," separate from you, or the physical world. It is everywhere and equally present. Its perfect Substance fills all space. It is within you. It is immersed in you as you are immersed in It. You are made of It. The Substance that created the planets, stars and galaxies is the same Substance that created you. You are Spirit/God Substance in expression. In fact, so is everyone and everything.

But I have a secret to tell you. (You may wish to close the blinds, draw the curtains and lock the doors! Take a couple of deep breaths and brace yourself. Are you ready?)

*You can use it.*

You can use this Higher Power to create, manifest and attract whatever you want in your life. In fact, you've been using it every day since you've had the ability and awareness to make your own choices, but which most likely you've had no idea you were doing so.

Every day, 24/7, from moment-to-moment, all the time.

Every time you hold or express a belief, make an assumption, think a thought, or utter a word, you are *using* this Power. You are "using" God.

You make up Its Mind.

You can make demands of It and you can direct It.

You can "command" God!

That's right, you read the above statements correctly. Now get ahold of yourself, take a few more deep breaths, calm down. Unlock your doors, open the curtains, raise the blinds, let in the light. You'll notice that lightning has not struck. The world has not come to an end. Neighbors with torches and pitchforks have not gathered outside and are pounding on your door.

"I can command God?? *Blasphemy!*" you may be thinking (or shouting). "Heresy! Woo-woo New age nonsense! Outrageous, unmitigated arrogance!"

Well perhaps so, if your idea of a Higher Power is that of a tyrannical old man with a white beard and volatile human qualities, foibles and emotions, who sits up in the clouds on a lofty throne looking down on us, his imperfect, flawed, lowly creations, and passes judgment on us with anger, whim and vindictiveness. (And, you might ask, what kind of a God would make flawed creations "in his own image," anyway, unless it, too, was flawed? Take a moment, if you dare, to consider that!)

If, on the other hand, your concept of a Higher Power is that of an infinite, universal, everywhere-present Creative Principle, Infinite Intelligence and Cosmic Consciousness that has created and loves Its creation unconditionally, always and impartially says "Yes!" and gives to us according to every belief we have, thought we think and word we speak, then the above statements are a profound, eye-opening truth. If you believe that this infinite, Divine Creative Source accepts Its creations equally and unconditionally without judgment, and is a Universal Power of good that lives, moves and has Its Being in, through and as us (and all Life), then the above statements not only make perfect sense, the idea that we can "make up" God's Mind (as human expressions that share Its attributes) is the highest, most amazingly loving gift that any ultimate Creator could give Its creation.

Yes! You can "use" God, "make up" Its Mind and even "command" It, without fear of Divine retribution, wrath, or eternal damnation (except as neutral Cause and Effect, which you set into motion). I am going to show you how.

# Commanding God

# or

# Making Up God's Mind

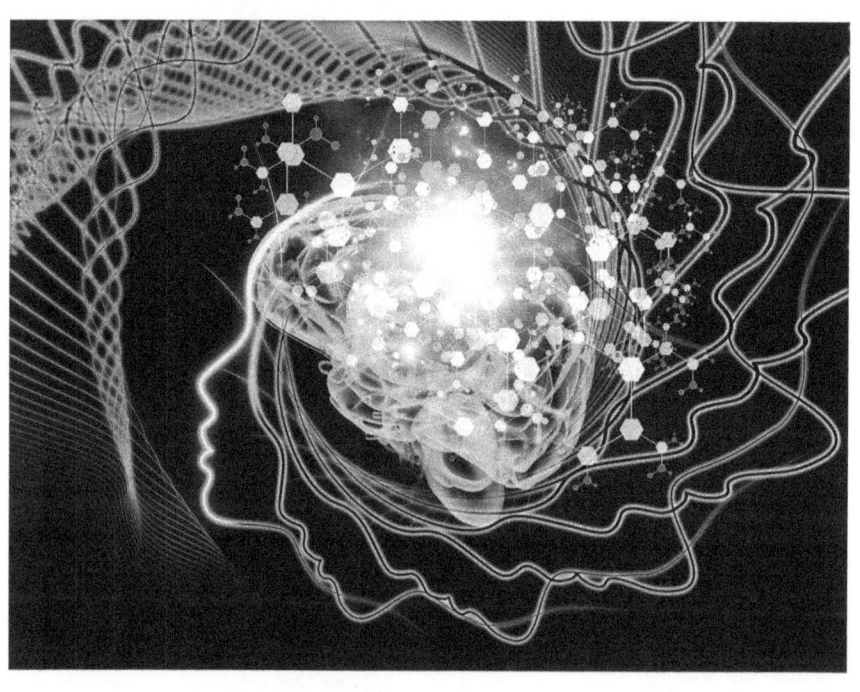

# PART ONE

# A MIND-BOGGLING REVELATION

*"...from [an] individual point of view…
universal creative power has no mind of its own…
therefore you can make up its mind for it."*

Thomas Troward
"The Edinburgh and Dore Lectures on Mental Science," 1904

The first time I read those words was for a metaphysical class I was taking. I was standing at the stove and nearly dropped the book into the frying pan. Had I read that right? "Universal creative power" (i.e. God) *has no mind of its own?* Therefore I could "make up its mind for it?" *God's Mind?* What "God" and what "mind" was Thomas Troward referring to here? Up until then I had never read, let alone conceived of, such an outrageous idea! And yet those words had been spoken and written over a century ago by one of the great pioneers of the late 19th/early 20th century New Thought movement, Judge Thomas Troward (1847-1916). The worldwide spiritual teaching known as Religious Science, or Science of Mind founded by Dr. Ernest Holmes in 1926, is Troward's most direct legacy.

Allowing Troward's statement to sink in, I was stunned to realize that as a student of spiritual metaphysics and mental science, and an individualized creation and expression of this "universal creative power," I was doing just that – making God's Mind up for It, or at least an *aspect* of God's Mind as it related to me (see below). What an audacious yet wonderfully revealing, and at the same time, humbling concept! According to this statement, every belief, idea and thought I had or word I spoke, every time I prayed, I was in fact "using" Spirit, "commanding" God, or setting into motion and giving direction to that intelligent but *mechanical and impersonal* aspect of God – the universal, subjective Law of Mind - that was responsible for taking what was impressed upon it and reflecting, manifesting, or out-picturing it back as form, condition or result in my life.

This meant that my words, backed by my beliefs, thoughts, ideas (and especially feelings) had power - the power to set this spiritual Law of Mind into motion and literally create my reality. Just as the physical universe is run by physical laws (like gravity), in back of these laws, and first and foremost, the universe is guided, directed, held together and run by *spiritual* laws.

This was an amazing, mind-boggling, wonderful – even freeing – truth to discover. Yet it also carried with it tremendous responsibility, once I became aware of the physical and spiritual results that what moved through my mind or came out of my mouth could potentially produce. It was also sobering to realize that if, in fact, I was responsible for creating my reality through what I believed, thought, said and felt, then I could no longer fall back on being a victim of circumstances or blaming others for things that happened to or around me. I couldn't even blame God, if in fact I was the one "making up" Its Mind! From this new understanding, I came to see that events actually happened *through* me, not *to* me. That also meant realizing that my life, up until and including that moment, was the result of my beliefs, my thinking, feelings and the choices I had made up to that point. (Ouch!) But knowing this also allowed me the freedom to now begin choosing differently, more consciously, mindfully, affirmatively, even assertively – to "use" God, direct or "make up" Its Mind, and even "command" It when necessary, in more positive, aware and constructive ways than I had up until then.

This book is a practical guide on how you can acquaint yourself with the Law of Mind and learn what it does; the creative power of your beliefs, thoughts, feelings and words, and learn to use them more effectively to consciously, assertively, positively and proactively create the kind of life you want, help avoid life's "train wrecks," or effectively handle and turn them around if they do occur.

There is an unlimited Intelligence, Consciousness and Force for creation in the universe that you also have within you, which you can use, and in so doing so transform your life!

*"...by a conscious mental use of the law of Mind, we can cause It to do definite things for us, through us. By conscious thinking, we give conscious direction to It."*
Ernest Holmes
"The Science of Mind" textbook

*"...through your intent you can literally command the laws of nature to fulfill your dreams and desires. As self-aware beings, we can command this organizing power through our conscious intent."*
Deepak Chopra
"The Seven Spiritual Laws of Success"

*Commanding God*

*Jon William Lopez, LSP*

# THE THREE ASPECTS OF GOD

Before moving forward into the processes and techniques presented in this book, it is important that the following clarification be made: when I state that you can "use," "make up" Its Mind, and even "command" God, I am in no way suggesting that as an individual you can run all of Infinite Spirit or the entire universe, like the Sorcerer's Apprentice who dreamed he could direct and manipulate the stars, planets, moons and tides. As stated previously, when I speak of "commanding" and "making up" God's Mind, I am talking about your ability, as an individual and a creative expression of Spirit, to use an *aspect* of It called Universal, Divine or Subjective Mind, to create your *personal* experience. Using this "Law of Mind," you direct and "knit" the unformed infinite, everywhere-present, universal, energetic *God-Substance* that already exists and which fills all space, but you do not actually create the Substance itself. You are made of it. You do the directing and the Law of Mind does the "knitting."

Although one indivisible, infinite Whole, God is "triune," or threefold in nature, having 3 aspects. The first and main aspect is, well, God/Spirit Itself - Infinite Intelligence, Universal Mind, Cosmic Consciousness, Higher Power, Creator, Source, whatever term you choose to call It. Within this first aspect exist the attributes of oneness, unity, wholeness, completeness, consciousness, awareness, volition, intention, creative will, action, ideas, knowing, omniscience, omnipotence, omnipresence, etc. It does not "contain" these attributes, It is ALL of these attributes. Your mind is an extension and aspect of the Universal Infinite Mind, which expresses in you, through you and as you on a finite, individualized level.

In using your mind, you put into effect the infinite Law of Mind. Although intelligent, this Law has no volition or "will" of its own. It is utterly impersonal and mechanically reflects or manifests back into form whatever is impressed, thought or said into it. Using this Law, which is as real, predictable, repeatable and scientifically accurate as any law of physics, is how you in fact "make up" God's Mind, how you can direct and "command" that aspect of Spirit on a personal, individual level. And so Troward's mind-boggling statement bears repeating:

> *"...universal creative power [the Law of Mind] has no mind of its own... therefore you can make up its mind for it."*

You do this with every thought you think, feeling you have, every word you speak, every belief you hold, and, by extension, by every choice you make and every action you take. In other words, your mind and thoughts are the cause, and your results and manifestations are the effect.

The Law of Mind works within the second aspect of God, which could also be called the soul, the "creative medium," "substance," "stuff" or "field" in which the Law of Mind does the actual manifesting of whatever is thought into or impressed upon it, and out of which physical form and conditions manifest. Attributes within this second aspect include creative medium, subconscious mind, unconscious mechanical action, the impersonal, passivity/receptivity, race consciousness, inherited characteristics, potential, possibility, spiritual prototypes (more on this later) and thought images.

Putting forth and releasing an intention, speaking a word, or having a belief, thought or feeling triggers and sets into motion the Law of Mind. Once triggered by Spirit, or by us *as* Spirit, it mechanically goes about the business of creating, manifesting, attracting or "reflecting back" as form the thing, condition, situation, or desire that was thought into it. It is impersonal, impartial and knows only to do what it's "told." Like the power of electricity, the Law of Mind can be used for either positive or negative purposes by anyone, and responds precisely to the thoughts and words that are backed by the beliefs and feelings we hold about them. Whether consciously or unconsciously, our thoughts, feelings, actions and beliefs create our experience and our reality. Whether we realize it or not, we "use" God this way every moment of every day. Also, our degree of belief, and the intensity of the feeling backing that belief, determines the nature, quality and strength of the results that are manifested for us.

The third aspect of God-Spirit is the physical plane, where the *cause* of our intention and desires is manifested into its *effect,* or form, situation or condition. It is within this field that time, space, matter, form, effect and result exist. This aspect includes the attributes of body, individualization, affairs, relationships, health, disease, desires, prosperity, abundance, lack, circumstances, conditions, appearances, situations and things.

God, Infinite Intelligence, is everywhere and equally present in all three of these aspects, and It "moves" through from pure intelligence, thought and volition into matter or form. It is no less present and powerful within each aspect, for It includes and is ALL of these aspects. What is true of It in the Infinite is equally as true of It in Its finite, physical expression, which includes the universe, you and me.

*Commanding God*

# Your Concept of God

As an introduction to our discussion on the ways and means you can "command" or "make up" God's Mind, it might be useful to first get clear on exactly how you perceive, experience and understand this Infinite, Creative Intelligence, as this determines your comfort level in being able to effectively use and direct It. "Using" Spirit depends on your image, perception, concept, or understanding of It, and whether you believe It's a "what," a "who," a "he" or a "she." Is It a person - male, female, or androgynous? Does He, She, or It have a body? Does it have a shape and/or a color(s)? Is It a thing, an idea, a concept, an energy or a force? Is It personal or impersonal? Is it kind and loving or stern, angry, judgmental, temperamental, or neutral? Is It all of these attributes or only some? What does It look like to you? Does It even have an appearance? And how comfortable are you with the idea of "making up" Its Mind, directing It, even "commanding" It, as well as in your own ability (and right) to do so?

Following is a revealing inner visualization-meditation process you can do to look at these questions. Read through it once or twice to familiarize yourself with the process, and then get comfortable, close your eyes, and go within. It is recommended that you be somewhere where you won't be disturbed or distracted.

*Jon William Lopez, LSP*

# MEDITATION-VISUALIZATION MY CONCEPT OF GOD

You might want to record this meditation in a calm, soothing voice and play it back, making it easier to go through. Or, read it section by section during the meditation process.

Take 3 deep, slow, cleansing breaths and with each exhalation become more and more relaxed. Go to that special inner space of the most high, that special "place" within you of your own creation where all is beautiful, perfect, quiet and safe. Visualize what this "place" or "space" looks like, what sounds you hear, and how it makes you feel. This is your innermost private, secret sanctuary, where you are well and at peace, safe and secure, where you can feel God's presence, hear Its "voice," and dialogue with It.

Now, gradually, create an image of God Itself before you. What does He/She/It look like? Does It have a shape or form at all? Does it have a color, smell, or texture? Is It abstract, tenuous, translucent, or solid? Does It shift its shape or remain constant? Is It human in appearance, male, female, or something else? Anything you see, or don't see, is exactly right for you. Take your time, allowing the images to easily and effortlessly evolve, take shape, come and go as they will. Notice if any resonate more with you than others. Do not censor yourself - let your imagination run free.

How do you feel being in Its presence? Do you feel separate or removed from It, or one with It? If you feel one with It, what does that feel like?

What qualities does It have? Is It kindly, loving, accepting, flexible? Or is It judgmental and stern? Dismissive or parental? Authoritative? Rigid? Unmoving? Indifferent or neutral? Just notice.

Are there any left-over concepts or images from past spiritual traditions or family upbringing that may be affecting what you're seeing or experiencing? If so, allow them to be there. Simply notice them and don't censor or judge.

Now, ask God to do something for you. Anything at all, simple or complicated, silly or stupid, serious or light. What is Its response? Does It say yes or no? Does It ridicule or dismiss you? Do you feel silly or stupid? Do you feel intimidated by asking? Presumptuous? Or do you feel confident, at ease in asking Spirit for something? Does asking It for something silly or trivial feel easier than asking It for something serious, important, big, or "heavy?" Spirit knows nothing of "big" or "little," "important," "heavy" or "serious,"

Now, instead of simply asking, change the language and the feeling behind it. Direct God to do something. *Command It!!* Be forceful and strong! Assert yourself and demand of It!

How does that feel? Do you feel afraid at having spoken to Spirit like this? Shocked? Presumptuous? Arrogant? Out of line? Afraid you've blasphemed and will be punished for such impudence? Does the audacity of a command make you feel embarrassed, silly, amused, or bemused at the very impudence of such a thing? And how does Spirit respond? Does Its response change from when you simply asked nicely, or remain the same? Is it angry, or happy, amused, loving? Or is It simply neutral? Does It do what you've commanded without pause, without a reaction of any kind? Does It simply say "yes, no problem," or "I'll take that under consideration," "yeah right!" or "how dare you!!" (If It says anything at all?)

Notice Its response. Notice yours.

Take a couple of deep breaths. Now easily and gently, bid farewell to and release your image, or images, of God, however it is that you have perceived It. Allow Its unconditional love and acceptance to envelop and soothe and warm you. All is well. It's all good. No harm has been done, least of all to God. Take another couple of deep breaths and become aware once again of your body and your outer surroundings. When you're ready, open your eyes.

*Jon William Lopez, LSP*

At this point you may wish to jot down a few words and thoughts about your meditation experience:

My concept or idea of God has:

Changed ___

Not changed ___

My idea or concept of God was:

_____
_____
_____
_____

It used to look like:

_____
_____
_____
_____

My idea or concept of God now is:

_____
_____
_____
_____

It now looks like:

_____
_____
_____
_____

*Commanding God*

It is: (easy, smooth, effortless, comfortable, powerful, etc.):
_____
_____
_____
_____to direct or "command" It.

I felt:
_____
_____
_____
_____

How I feel now about my ability to "use," "command" God, or "make up" Its Mind:
_____
_____
_____
_____

Any additional conclusions, insights, surprises, or revelations I had, if any:
_____
_____
_____
_____

    Are you ready now to start creating and manifesting your Life's desires? God awaits your commands!

*Jon William Lopez, LSP*

*Commanding God*

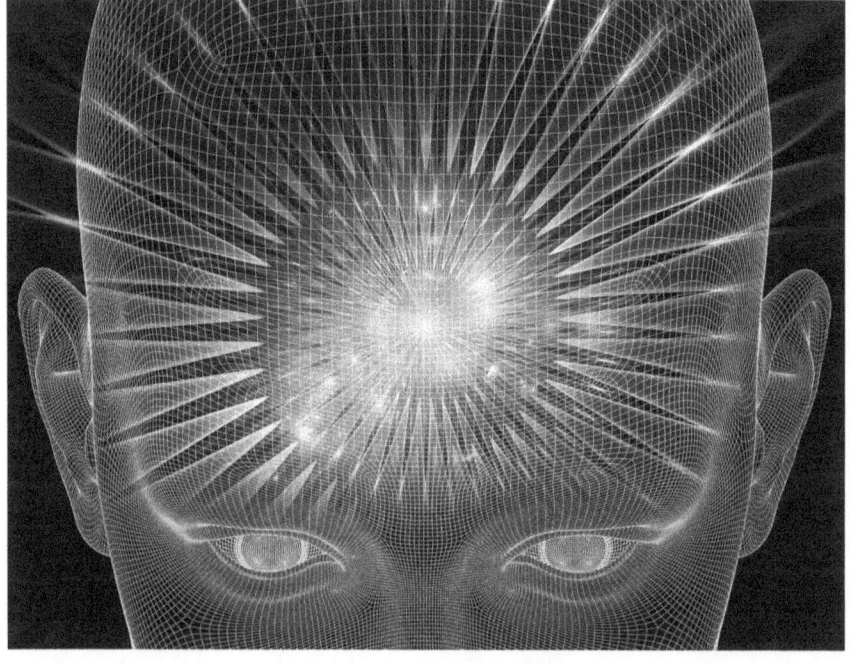

# PART TWO

# COMMANDING GOD CONCEPTS

So now that you are clearer about and hopefully feel a bit more comfortable with your image of or idea of God (and how to relate to It), here are some useful concepts to consider and keep in mind as you start on your path towards consciously "commanding" Infinite Intelligence and "making up" Its Mind with awareness and intention.

### COMMANDING CONCEPT 1:

### HOW MUCH GOOD (GOD) CAN YOU BELIEVE IN?

In addition to your concept of God, your effectiveness in "making up" Its Mind is dependent on how aware you are of Its presence within you, around you and Its *ability to manifest for you*. Since Spirit can only do *for* you what It can do *through* you, it is up to you to decide how much God, or good, you can allow yourself to accept, believe in and ask for. *The Universe responds to you always according to your belief.* If you believe Spirit is limited and that you as an expression of It can create only a little in life, the Universe will impartially comply and you will most likely get just a little. Whereas, if you believe you live in, are part of and can accept the *unlimited, infinite* abundance and good from a Universe that always says *yes!* and whose access to that abundance is your divine natural birthright, available to you right here and now, you can have exactly that. Putting limits on an unlimited Creative Intelligence is a belief in your *own* limitation that will manifest and out-picture as limitation and lack in your life.

Recognizing and *knowing* that you have at your disposal and are a part, creation, and expression of an infinite, endless Source will manifest riches (and not just material ones) in your life. The quality and sum total of your life now is the result (the cause and effect) of your past and present attitudes, beliefs and assumptions. They determine the boundaries and set the limits to what your manifestations look like in the physical world.

How much God can you believe in? How much Good? And do you believe you can manifest it? That you have the ability to do so? Do you believe you are worthy of manifesting it?

## COMMANDING CONCEPT 2:

### CAUSE, EFFECT, SPACE AND (AS A RESULT) TIME

The Universal Creative Intelligence we call God, Spirit, Source, Higher Power, etc., is the ultimate First Cause of everything that exists, all creation, all Life. When It wills, thinks or "moves" within Itself, a resulting outcome or "effect" follows, such as a condition, circumstance, or a physical out-picturing into form (two or more of which creates physical separation, distinction and space). For every outcome or physical manifestation (effect) there is an underlying physical or spiritual origin (cause) back of it. Like this Creative Intelligence, what we believe, think, feel, say and do are the "causes" which set the Law of Mind into motion. The results we get back are the "effects" of those beliefs, thoughts, feelings, words and actions. Our world, our present personal life situation, our experience now at this very moment, are the results or effects that have manifested over time as individuals and collectively as a species. For every action, thought, idea, belief or word we express there is an opposite and equal re-action, response, result or consequence. Our beliefs, thoughts and actions now in the present moment will manifest as our future! The physical universe, everything around us (and in us) now are the results/effects of an infinite number of causes stretching back through "time," a never-ending process that will also stretch infinitely into the "future."

In actuality, there's no such physical thing as "time." It does not exist as a separate physical reality, entity or "thing." There is no concrete "future" except what we can imagine now, or "past" except what we mentally remember and what has been physically written down or recorded. "Time" is an abstract concept, a means of measurement created by our minds and memories. "It" helps us to keep track of what we've done, where we've been, what has happened, place into context, and what we may, would like, or intend to do in an imagined, potential, but not yet created "future." "Time" is a mental construct we use to measure, keep track of and record movement through space on this physical plane. In reality, "now" is all there is. All thought, experience, creation and all reality on the physical plane happens *now* and exists only now in an ever-present, constant continuum. When we think about the past, we are thinking about it *now*. When we imagine, plan for, or think about the future, we are doing so *now*. God, Spirit, Higher Power, Infinite Intelligence, Cosmic Consciousness (call It what you will), being an infinite, complete oneness, an absolute all-ness, wholeness and totality, everywhere and equally present and filling all space, is all there is. As such, It knows nothing *of* space, distance, or separation and is therefore "timeless."

A fascinating concept to meditate on is the idea that in the absolute, infinite, all-ness, wholeness and *completeness* of Spirit, every event that has happened, could have happened, is happening now, could happen now, and ever will or could happen in the future is *already present and simultaneously in existence now*, all at once, just like recorded data already exists in its entirety on a hard drive, flash drive, CD/DVD, Cloud, iPod/Pad, tablet (or vinyl phonograph record or magnetic tape for those of us ancient enough to remember), and is only waiting to be accessed, processed, perceived, experienced, or linearly "played" in the now. What direction we take or what we choose to "play" is up to us, but the consequences of the choices and resulting paths are already laid out.

On the other hand, if we are creating our experience moment by moment, then events in the "future" are NOT already laid out, written in stone, and do not pre-exist, except as *potential or possibility*. With each new choice we make and action we take, a whole new set of possible and potential outcomes and "futures" are created or discarded depending on the paths we take. Once an action is taken or an event occurs, it immediately becomes the "past" and is "written in stone," so to speak, for it cannot be changed (at least not by us on this physical plane).

It therefore follows that whatever we "make up" God's Mind to do is also created *now* as a spiritual prototype on the spiritual plane, the moment it is asked for and "commanded." It just might take a little "time" to transition to and manifest on this physical plane, which consists of individualized form, space, and consequently, "time."

## COMMANDING CONCEPT 3:
## BELIEVE IT AND YOU'LL SEE IT -
## THE POWER OF YOUR BELIEFS, THOUGHTS AND WORDS

You, like all of Life, are a perfect expression, manifestation, out-picturing and individualization of Spirit. Like all of Creation, you are made of perfect God-Substance. Like a fish in water, you are immersed in It and It is immersed in you. There is no separation, only a differentiation of frequency and vibration of the same energy.

If you accept that Spirit not only created you but lives and expresses in you, through you, as you and *is* you, then it follows that Its Mind, in the Infinite, is your mind on a finite level, just as a rose blossom is part of the rosebush, an ocean wave is part of the ocean, or a ray of sunlight is a projection of the sun. All the elements and attributes of the Source are present in and part of the out-pictured form. Therefore, what is true of Spirit is true of you! You are created in Its "likeness" and "image." Like God's, on an individual level your thoughts and words have power! Backed and powered by the degree of your belief, they can and do create. They are Law in the Universe! When you make up *your* mind or set an intention whether in thought, word, or deed, consciously or unconsciously, positively or negatively, you are in effect "making up" Subjective Mind too - directing and "commanding" It, because your mind and Its Mind are one and the same, only on different levels and at different scales. (Subjective Mind is that part of the second attribute of Spirit: Soul, or God Substance, which unquestioningly and without judgement or evaluation, takes the impress of your thought and, like a hand-print in sand, goes about the business of manifesting it.)

Through the Law of Mind and the Law of Cause and Effect, the Universe always out-pictures back to you exactly what you believe, think, and say into It, which is why your "reality," although appearing to be objective, always seems to be just the way you *personally believe* it to be (yet may not be that way for someone else).

You see, you manifest and experience your reality because you believe it to be that way first, not the other way around. What you believe to be true within is what you will consequently see and experience without. You see *from the context* of what you believe. To change anything on the physical plane, first change how you "see" it within yourself. Ultimately, you perceive from Spirit and out-picture that awareness into reality.

## COMMANDING CONCEPT 4:
## SPIRIT DOESN'T MOVE UNTIL YOU MOVE IT

Ready for another mind-boggling concept? No need to close the curtains for this one (unless you want to).

*Spirit doesn't move until you move it.*

*"We live in a universe of Infinite Substance and numberless forms, wherein nothing is moved unless Intelligence moves it."*
Ernest Holmes

From your personal level, nothing is manifested and nothing within the universe is "moved" until you move it, or set it in motion.

Seriously? God doesn't move until Intelligence (you) *moves It?*

*Precisely.* Where *you* are concerned, the Law of Mind does not "move" (i.e. take action, create or manifest) unless you, as an intelligent free-willed creation of Spirit, "moves" It—that is, triggers It, directs It, sets an intention, puts the Law of Mind into motion. Now of course Infinite Intelligence, on an absolute universal scale, is always in motion, creating, maintaining, sustaining and animating Life, the planets, stars, galaxies (and who knows how many universes). It set your body in motion and continues to create, animate and sustain it moment by moment, continuously. That's not what I mean. What I am saying is that from an individual personal level, Universal Creative Intelligence, the Law of Mind, is rather like electricity – it hums along not doing much in particular until you *direct it and put It to use.* And because it is impersonal, it has no agenda or intention of its own. It can be used to light a city, set a tree on fire, or shock you (or worse). The volition, will and intention comes from you!

We have all asked, at one time or another, what God wants us to do, or what Its will or "plan" for us is. The truth is, *the Universe "wants" what we tell It we want!* It's always ready and available to do our bidding, whether it be conscious or unconscious, positive or negative. Whatever we think into It, the Law of Mind responds with an unbiased, impartial, unequivocal "Yes!"

> *"Creative Mind of Itself has no specific intention as far as individuals are concerned. We give It the only intention It has for us."*
> Ernest Holmes
> Living the Science of Mind

> *"How do we know what the intention of the Universal Mind may be? It has no intention because it is impersonal...it will no more oppose us by specific plans of its own than will steam or electricity."*
> Thomas Troward
> The Edinburgh and Dore Lectures on Mental Science

Spirit has no pre-planned agenda for us. We may not know at the time when or how what we've asked for or affirmed will come into fruition, but God does. It's not our business, it's Spirit's! Once *we* speak and release our word, the Law of Mind immediately, automatically and neutrally goes about the business of creating the perfect ways and means of manifesting our desire.

This amazing idea is based on the truth that this Universal Creative Intelligence is not a personality (a separate humanlike entity with human whims and emotions), but a *principle*. It is an infinite, conscious, universal, cosmic creative power and force that, through Subjective Mind, intelligently responds proportionally to the energy (thought, word, feeling or action) that is directed into It. It unconditionally yet impersonally responds to, and reflects back to us whatever it is that we believe about It, think into It and say about It (and therefore, by extension, ourselves). Being receptive but impersonal, the Law of Mind always says "yes!" and does not "move" until we move It!

## COMMANDING CONCEPT 5:
### POLAR OPPOSITES

*Do you believe your beliefs?*

As stated earlier, you use the Law of Mind on a daily, moment-by-moment basis whether you're aware of it or not. But just think what you could do if you were always aware of this Law and used it in a mindful, directed, conscious, proactive manner! Your very method of thinking would change. Knowing that your core beliefs, assumptions, thoughts, feelings and words continuously create your reality would change your thought processes on a profound level. Do you believe your beliefs? Are they objectively true? At every moment, you would come to watch and become aware of every belief you hold, thought you think, feeling you have, and word you speak, knowing the effect they could produce, and whether this would serve you or not. You would learn to notice every negative belief or thought and turn it around to its positive *polar opposite* before ever opening your mouth to speak. This, of course, would take mindful practice, but after awhile it could become second nature.

When you catch yourself having a negative thought, thank your mind for sharing and then release it, replacing it with its positive opposite. For example, if the thought "I am useless and incompetent." enters your mind, immediately say to yourself "Thank you for sharing, mind (or ego), but that is not the truth. I am in fact a perfect creation and expression of Infinite Intelligence (God, Spirit, etc.) and Its Mind is my Mind now. Because I am here I am useful and important. I am competent in everything I do." (A quicker way to do this might be to immediately say to yourself "Cancel, cancel!" in response to the negative thought and then state its positive polar opposite.)

Following are some other common negative statements and their polar opposites:

Negative Thought: I'm not smart about money.

Polar Opposite: God's Mind is my mind, and Infinite Intelligence expresses as me at all times. Money is God-energy and everything I need to know about handling and circulating it responsibly and intelligently is revealed and available to me now.

Short version: Money is God-energy and I use it wisely at all times for my greatest good.

NT: Money is scarce and difficult to earn.

PO: Money is limitless God-energy and as I attune and align myself with the infinite abundance of the Universe with which I am One, it flows to me easily and effortlessly. I always have more than enough money to meet all my needs.

Short version: There is no lack of money in the world and I easily and gratefully claim, attract and manifest my rightful share now!

Short version 02: All my financial needs are met now and at all times!


NT: I'm afraid to meet people/make friends.

PO: Recognizing the Spirit in myself and in others, I realize there is nothing to fear. We are all one. I easily attract people of like mind and make friends effortlessly. I am the friend I wish to attract.

Short version: I attract people of like mind and am the friend I wish to have.


NT: I'm clumsy and unattractive.

PO: I'm a perfect, graceful and beautiful expression of Spirit within as well as without. I move with grace and ease.

Short version: I'm a graceful, beautiful, perfect expression of God.


NT: I have no purpose in life/I don't know what my purpose is.

PO: As a perfect expression of Spirit, I recognize that my purpose is whatever I choose and declare it to be! I live life fully doing whatever I love and makes my heart sing!

Short version: Doing what I love to do is my purpose in life.

NT: I am confused and don't know what to do/how to proceed in this situation.

PO: God always shows me what to do, how to do it and when, in ways I can clearly see, know, understand and easily take action on for perfect results and outcome.

PO 02: God always guides me, leads me and shows me the way. Each step I take reveals the next. I am on my perfect path.

Short Version: God is always with me and shows me the perfect ways, means and solutions to this situation.


NT: I'm not smart/resourceful enough to make a good living/support myself.

PO: God always supports Its expression. The infinite, all-knowing Intelligence of Universal Mind is my mind now and reveals to me all the ways I can support myself easily, fully and prosperously.

Short version: I am divinely equipped with everything necessary to support myself in every way.

Short version 02: God always supports Its expression. My needs are always met.


NT: I don't have what it takes to make it in life. I am flawed.

PO: I am a perfect expression and out-picturing of a perfect Creator. Everything It is I am. I come pre-wired with everything and have all the skills I need to get along and "make it" in life easily, effortlessly, successfully, intelligently and joyfully!

Short version: Because I am God Itself in perfect expression, I come divinely equipped and have all it takes to make it in every area and aspect of my life!

NT: I'm not lovable/nobody loves me.

PO: As a perfect creation of the one Divine Loving Source, which completely and unconditionally accepts and loves all Its creation, I recognize that I am loved and accepted unconditionally. The very fact that I exist makes me lovable and capable of loving. As I freely and unconditionally love, I am loved in return.

Short Version: I am a perfect expression of God, which loves me unconditionally, and the love I give returns to me multiplied.

Try making a game of it. After awhile, positive, supportive thoughts will begin to outnumber the negative ones, and may soon be the first ones that come into your mind instead of the last.

Your mind was not created for negativity, but as an impartial instrument for you to use for your highest and greatest good. A way I've been practicing dealing with and counteracting negative self-talk is to immediately say to myself "God bless you!" instead of "You idiot!" or similar self-deprecating statement. Try doing this yourself.

*Commanding God*

# PART THREE

## COMMANDING GOD: TWO POWERFUL AND EFFECTIVE WAYS AND MEANS FOR MAKING UP ITS MIND

The previous section discussed some of the important ideas to keep in mind and hold in your consciousness in preparation for "making up" God's Mind. Now we come to some practical techniques and tools for doing so, beginning with what are probably the two most basic and powerful spiritual tools there are:

### AFFIRMATIONS AND AFFIRMATIVE PRAYER
### (OR SPIRITUAL MIND TREATMENT)

Your mind, being an aspect of Infinite Mind, broadcasts a powerful field of energy! Your thoughts and words, backed by your underlying consciousness (beliefs) and fueled by your feelings, are magnetic. They emanate from you into the universal Substance and the Law of Mind, where subsequently Subjective Mind receives and intelligently (but mechanically and impersonally) processes them to reflect back, out-picture, manifest, create and draw to you, like a handprint in sand, whatever you've impressed upon it. This is a constant, ongoing, moment-by-moment, never-ending activity. With the tools of Affirmations and Affirmative Prayer, you can use and direct this mental energy in a conscious, aware, positive, proactive, assertive, and yes, commanding manner!

## AFFIRMATIONS

You've all heard of them (and if you're reading this book) have probably used them yourself at one time or another, with varying degrees of purpose and intensity (as well as results). Affirmations are generally short, positive statements of truth, or a truth you would like to see manifested in your life. Affirmations are:

- Short and to the point – the idea is stated in 1, 2, or 3 sentences.
- Always in the present tense, as if your statement is a reality now.
- Delivered with positive emotion, confidence, faith, feeling and belief. An affirmation is a truth about *you*, a situation, condition, or thing, no ifs ands or buts.

When it comes to affirming (as well as in Affirmative Prayer), there are six major areas that people deal with in their lives:

1. abundance and prosperity (money, abundant life)
2. health (wellness, illness, dis-ease)
3. love (relationships, friendships, self-love)
4. purpose (work, career, vocation)
5. self-expression (creativity, calling, the arts)
6. loss (change, loss of things, loved-ones, pets, "death")

Following are examples of simple one, two, or three-sentence affirmations for each of these issues:

- Prosperity: Spirit is all there is and It is unlimited. As a perfect expression of Spirit, I live in and am one with an infinitely abundant Universe. Within this infinitude I lack for nothing and all my needs are prosperously and abundantly met at all times.
- Health: I am a whole, complete expression, out-picturing and manifestation of a perfect Creator, patterned after a divine, whole and perfect blueprint. It expresses and out-pictures in me and as me as vibrant, perfect physical health, wellness, high energy, wholeness and joyful well-being. Perfect good health is my divine and natural state now and always. I am whole and complete.

I am perfect, healthy, whole and complete.

- Love: God is total unconditional love, acceptance, and complete allowing-to-be. As a perfect expression of this Divine Loving Source, I recognize that I am wholly, completely and unconditionally loved and accepted by God and everyone around me. As I love, it returns to me multiplied!

God loves me unconditionally and I am loved by others.

- Purpose: Spirit always supports Its expression. As a perfect manifestation of Spirit, I realize that the fact that I am alive reveals that I have a divine reason for being here and I get to create it. My purpose is revealed to me and expressed through perfect, joyful, satisfying and fulfilling activity and work that I love doing. My purpose is doing whatever brings me joy!
- Self-expression: As a perfect out-picturing and expression of the one Universal Cosmic Creator, which always seeks to express through and as Its creation, I allow my God-given talents and creativity to flow through me and express in all good, satisfying and fulfilling ways now.
- Loss: God-Spirit is always unified, whole and complete. It is all there is, therefore nothing is ever lost or separate from It. What appears to be "lost" to me is now revealed, found, restored, or replaced with something better by my right of consciousness.

- <u>Loss (of a loved one)</u>: God-Spirit is always one, unified, whole and complete Life force. It is all there is, therefore nothing or no one can ever be separate from or "lost" within It. Life, energy and consciousness can never be destroyed, only transformed, and are thus eternal. My cherished loved one, although no longer expressing on this physical plane, is not lost. He/she has transitioned to a higher, better and freer form of expression, forever growing, joyfully expanding and evolving.

Stated with positive emotion, energy, feeling and with faith and trust in their outcome, affirmations are powerful, to-the-point statements that, given time and space to work (the physical universe must arrange itself to bring about the necessary conditions for you, which already exist in Spirit) are efficient, effective ways to manifest a desired situation, thing, condition, or outcome. They are always stated in the present tense and declared as if they are already true for you now (which triggers the Law of Mind into getting busy!). Repeated often with confidence, conviction and enthusiasm (aloud is very effective), their power accumulates, with the corresponding results.

Use affirmations only for your own positive benefit, to create only good for yourself or others. Why would you wish anything different? Your beliefs, thoughts and words create a magnetic, vibrational aura around you, which not only colors your perceptions, it attracts events and people of similar ilk (the Law of Attraction). Remember, what you put out you get back. Cause and effect. A negative belief, thought or word is just as much an "affirmation" to Subjective Mind as a positive one is! Refuse to focus on or entertain any belief, thought or word of negativity, pessimism, judgment, fear, prejudice, hate, lack or limitation. Despite appearances or conditions to the contrary, hold steadfast in an attitude that everything is for your highest and best good and growth.

Write some strong, assertive affirmations below. If and when you can, speak them aloud with conviction, as if they were true now, and notice how you feel. Consider keeping an affirmation journal.

Perfect Health

_____
_____
_____
_____

Abundance/Prosperity

_____
_____
_____
_____

Love/Relationships

_____
_____
_____
_____

Work/Job

_____
_____
_____

Well-being, Peace of Mind

_____
_____
_____
_____

Loss/Change

_____
_____
_____
_____

Affirmations aren't just for "big" and "heavy" stuff. They can of course be used for seemingly "smaller" more everyday situations as well. For example:

- I look forward to this day with ease, happiness and joy.
- I quickly, easily and effortlessly get to work on time.
- I ace this day!
- I move through this day easily, smoothly and pleasantly.
- I accomplish everything I need to do today easily, smoothly and joyfully.
- My flight/trip is easy, pleasurable, smooth, uneventful and safe.
- I arrive safely at my destination.
- I perform this task/ job perfectly, easily, effortlessly, competently and professionally.
- I am perfect Spirit, perfect Mind and perfect Body.
- God shows me exactly what to do, how to do it and when.
- God shows me exactly what to do in this/any/every situation now.
- God creates perfect outcome in this situation.
- All unfolds in divine right timing and action.
- No matter what the present appearance, situation, or circumstance, God is always there.
- All my needs are met!

- I am perfect health and wholeness.
- God/Spirit is within me, above me, below me and all around me. It surrounds me.
- God/Spirit always supports, sustains, supplies, guides and guards me.
- I am immersed in Spirit as It is immersed in me.
- I am made of perfect, healing, divine God-substance. It continuously creates, animates, heals, sustains and perfects every atom, molecule, cell, fiber, tissue and organ of my being. I am perfect, healthy, whole and complete.

## AFFIRMATIVE PRAYER/SPIRITUAL MIND TREATMENT

Perhaps the most effective method I've found for directing my powerful mental energy, "making up" God's Mind or "commanding" It, and having it produce the highest desired results is through the technique of Affirmative Prayer, also called Spiritual Mind Treatment. The latter term, coined by Ernest Holmes, founder of the Science of Mind teaching, originates from the idea that, as a physician treats a patient physically, an affirmative prayer practitioner "treats" an individual on a mental and spiritual level in a similar fashion for the purpose of healing - physically, mentally or spiritually. Spiritual Mind Treatment or Affirmative Prayer differs from traditional prayer, which seeks help and supplication from an entity "out there" with the hope that if it so pleases this separate entity, the request might or might not be granted. Affirmative Prayer/Spiritual Mind Treatment, on the other hand, makes a strong, positive, affirmative, present-tense declaration for a desired outcome, circumstance, condition or thing, with the complete and utter belief, faith, conviction, trust and feeling that whatever is declared or asked for *already exists* as a divine spiritual potential, prototype, blueprint or idea in the quantum Infinite Mind, waiting to be physically manifested. As a spiritual potential, it is already given. No supplication is required and no deals need to be made (nor can they be) with God. Our strong intention and mindful, directed use of our words, backed by a clear consciousness, sincere, trusting, positive belief and feeling, are what do the trick. Coming from the knowing that everything is already readily available to us from an infinite, unlimited Source, we direct or "command" the Law of Mind to reveal and produce our good for us, giving grateful thanks in advance, knowing that its manifestation is assured according to and *as* our belief.

Affirmative Prayer/Spiritual Mind Treatment does not will results to happen, but provides a mental/spiritual opening and receptivity within the one treating to *allow* manifestation to happen. Proof that the spiritual laws set into motion by the prayer have worked is *demonstrated* by the manifestation. A "demonstration" is the outward result of this prayer process working.

There is an important factor to be mindful of. Indeed, the Universe always says *yes,* but more than reflecting back to us what we superficially think into it, it actually manifests what's in *and from the deeper consciousness and core beliefs* we have. In other words, we can affirm and pray for something we want, but if we're holding a deep-down belief in its polar opposite (i.e. praying for prosperity and abundance when in truth we actually hold a core belief and consciousness of poverty, lack, or limitation), then *we will manifest the core belief*, i.e. an "abundance" of poverty, lack or limitation. A true abundance consciousness, on the other hand, manifests as more abundance, while a consciousness of lack creates more lack. Whatever you look at and focus on, you get more of. Although we may be praying *for* a specific thing, our results will always be affected by where we are actually praying *from* (our subjective subconscious).

> *"Though we don't always get what we're looking and praying for, we do always get what we're looking and praying from. What you see from is what you get...the context of our consciousness always [affects] its content."*
> Rev. Noel McInnis
> "Embodying God's Faith:
> The Company God Keeps and How to Keep It," Article, 2012

So when you affirm or pray, be mindful of what you are really asking for. If you pray for a brand new sports car, more money in the bank, perfect health, a romantic relationship, or the perfect job, is that what you really want? Superficially, on a physical level, perhaps yes. But what is the *spiritual principle* in back of those things? Underlying the condition, situation or thing, *you are praying for consciousness, not conditions!* For example, in praying for that special car, what you're wanting to experience is that you're really a free, mobile, unrestricted, abundant being living in an open, unlimited universe. A prayer for a soulmate could be to know you're lovable and want to be cherished, appreciated and validated; a desire for connection with someone of like mind, a desire to be seen and heard. Praying for the perfect job – to feel useful, be of service, doing what you're here to do, fully self-expressing. Having more money – feeling supported, secure, sustained, supplied, unrestricted, unlimited, abundant, prosperous, free. Perfect health – living your best life freely, joyfully, without restriction or limitation.

You can manifest the conditions, but if you don't also create the underlying consciousness, you will be ever seeking more conditions. If you have the underlying consciousness, however, the conditions will usually manifest automatically (or if they don't, you'll still be secure in your wholeness).

## PRE-PRAYING: GETTING INTO THE "MODE"

Before stating (silently or aloud) or giving any affirmation or affirmative prayer, I recommend the following steps. They will help prepare your consciousness for the best results possible as you effectively use, direct, and "command" God:

- Relax your body and quiet your mind. If possible, go somewhere where you're not likely to be interrupted. Ideally this would be in a quiet corner of your room, or a place/space you've specifically designated for meditation. It could be outside in nature, in your home, or even at the office, if you can spare a few minutes undisturbed. Preferably sitting, take a few deep, slow breaths and gradually relax your body from head to toe. Mentally repeat a mantra or say an affirmation for calmness, openness and receptivity. Extraneous thoughts will bubble up, that's natural. Allow them to come and go with ease. As you continue to focus on your breath and/or your mantra, these thoughts will gradually recede into the background, become quieter and less obtrusive.

- Put yourself in a place of deservedness. This can be in the form of an affirmation. As a perfect expression of Spirit, the resources of the cosmos are at your command, are your divine birthright and you deserve as much good as you are willing to claim and accept. You deserve and are divinely entitled to as much good as you can imagine and believe!

- Believe you have the power and ability to create what you want. Know that your word is powerful and creative. It is God speaking through and as you! It is Law in the Universe! The Law of Mind "hears" your word, receives it and knows what to do, how to do it, and when. This power and ability is within you – you came pre-wired with it and you have everything you need now to manifest your good. The more convinced you are of the power of your word, the more power your word will have!

- Get clear on what you want. State in one or two clear, concise sentences what your desire or intention, thing, situation, circumstance or condition you wish to manifest is. Be as specific as possible and narrow it down to its simplest form, idea or essence/spiritual principle. Getting clear on your desire establishes in your mind (and in Divine Mind) the idea, concept, or thing that you will be affirming and focusing on later, giving the Universe a preview, so to speak, of what you'll be asking of It. Remember, the Law of Mind takes you literally. Writing it down is also effective, as this helps solidify it in your consciousness. A vague idea will produce vague, lesser results, whereas a concrete, clear idea will produce stronger results. See it as already a reality!

- Use your imagination! Your imagination is one of your most powerful and transcendent faculties. Spiritual teacher Neville Goddard considered the imagination to be God within us. (More about him in Part 5.) It is the mental field of potential and possibility, God-energy and Substance Itself, out of which is created all manifestation and from which comes all form. If it comes easily to you, visualize your desire as already manifested. Create a strong, clear image of it in your mind, as if its real and already so. Any clear, vivid, detailed mental image persistently held in mind results in an actual experience in accordance with that image. Imagining or visualizing the desired result gives it a much greater degree of reality in your consciousness and a sense that it exists *now*.

- As you visualize and use your imagination, feelings will come up. This is very important! Feelings are the fuel of your prayer! The feelings you get from imagining your desire as already real give your treatment that much more of a sense of reality, presence and certainty because your mind and body respond to feelings. Let those feelings saturate you, filling every cell of your being, from head to toe, and allow yourself to deeply experience your demonstration as if it were already a reality in your life. Feeling as though your desire is already fulfilled tells the Universe that your request is already a reality and triggers It into manifesting your wish. (Imagination and feelings are discussed in more detail further on.)

- Know what you're going to do with your demonstration, how you're going to use it or live it once it manifests. Along with getting clear on what it is you want, knowing how you're going to actually use your good takes the process of getting clear a step further. It gives your demonstration a solid, concrete purpose and direction.

- Disregard outward appearances, conditions, the opinions of others, the past and the future. Before and while affirming or praying, don't allow present circumstances, situations, appearances or conditions affect, influence, or weaken your resolve or pollute your consciousness. Remain focused on and be steadfast in your present desire and intention. Remember, Principle (God) has no precedent, meaning that just because something happened a certain way before, it doesn't have to be the same way again. God knows only NOW, and where It is concerned, all things are created anew in the present moment from a Universe of infinite potential, possibility and solution.

Meditate on and hold the above ideas in your consciousness until you feel ready to proceed.

Ready? Set?

*"Command ye Me!"*

God

A full-blown Affirmative Prayer or Spiritual Mind Treatment consists of several different steps, which takes it beyond a simple affirmation, and makes it deeper, more thorough, powerful and complete. Like an affirmation, Treatment declares, asserts and affirms with faith, belief, confidence and conviction in no uncertain terms that whatever result is desired is already a given, here and now, done. The reason for this declaration of certainty is because we live in an infinite universal creative medium of infinite possibility, where all outcomes or results already exist *in spiritual potentiality,* ready and "waiting" to be triggered into manifestation. Released into the Law of Mind, an Affirmative Prayer or Treatment moves within and "harnesses" or "grasps" this potential and possibility, imprinting itself onto God-substance/Subjective Mind like a hand-print in sand, where it is transformed into what is called a "mental equivalent," thought image, blueprint, or idea, of what is desired. A Treatment ends with a statement of gratitude and thanksgiving for the gift that is thus already a perfect idea in Cosmic Consciousness. It is then released into the Law of Mind, which takes over and goes about the business of bringing the desired idea or mental equivalent into physical manifestation.

An Affirmative Prayer need not have a specific outline. Like a shorter affirmation, it is a longer, more detailed positive declaration (as in Step 3 of a Spiritual Mind Treatment, described below) in the present tense of a truth, desire, condition, situation or thing you would like to manifest or experience. Just like a more structured Spiritual Mind Treatment, this declaration also goes out into the Law of Mind and is reflected back to you as form, situation or condition.

However, as created by Ernest Holmes in the Science of Mind teaching, a Spiritual Mind Treatment is a more structured and complete affirmative declaration that has five (or in some versions, seven) steps.

The five steps of a complete Spiritual Mind Treatment are:

1. Recognition
2. Unification
3. Declaration or Realization (within which could be included the sub-steps of Denial and Re-affirmation)

4. Thanksgiving
5. Release

**Step 1, Recognition**: Acknowledges that there is an infinite, universal, intelligent, creative Higher Power, God, Spirit, Cosmic Consciousness, Creator, Source of all Life, etc. which lives, moves, expresses, out-pictures and has Its Being in, through and as Its creation, as all Life. It is all there is and It is everywhere and equally present. In this first step, the God-attributes or principles you are treating for can also be stated (i.e. "God is...").

**Step 2, Unification**: Recognizes that what is true of this Creative Intelligence/Spirit must also be true of Its expression, which naturally includes you. What is true of God is true of you. Spirit lives, moves and has Its Being in, through and as you, because It *is* you. It is your source and you are one with it and of It.

**Step 3, Declaration (or Realization)**: You recognize that, possessing the same attributes as Spirit, your word, like Spirit's, has the power to create. It is Law in the Universe! And so you declare in a positive, directed, affirmative, even assertive or forceful (commanding) manner, in the present tense, with confidence, faith, feeling and conviction, exactly what result, condition, situation, or thing you desire. Within this step, the sub-step of Denial refers to any negative, unwanted condition, fear, blockage or false belief you may have (consciously or not) as not having any further power or influence in or over your consciousness, and is totally and completely released. There is nothing within or without you blocking the manifestation of your desire! Following is Re-affirmation, which re-states the good you are treating for. You state it as already given, already done and you have it now.

**Step 4, Thanksgiving**: You give thanks and express gratitude, knowing that what you are affirming is already yours not only in Divine Mind as a perfect idea, mental equivalent or spiritual blueprint of what you desire, but also a physical reality in your experience.

**Step 5, Release**: In which the prayer or treatment you have just given is let go and released into Mind, allowing the Law to do its work. This is a very important step, since what you are putting into motion must be released and allowed to process. Although there is no "time" in Spirit, it sometimes does take processing on the physical plane for your treatment to manifest, as the Universe arranges Itself to bring about, manifest or attract the condition, circumstance or thing you've asked for. By stating and releasing your word, you've planted a divine seed. Be patient and allow it to germinate. You can't dig up a seed you've planted (which is what a prayer is) to see if it's growing. It must be allowed to germinate, do its thing without interruption, so that it can sprout. So it is with your affirmative prayer.

Following are examples of a complete Spiritual Mind Treatment, each of which use the above 5 steps:

## Treatment for Abundance

Recognition:

There is only one Power, one Presence, one Divine Loving Source. Its Divine Substance is everywhere present and fills all space. It is Spirit, God, the Creator of all Life and is the infinite, limitless supplier of all prosperity, good and abundance.

Unification:

Recognizing myself as a creation and part of God's Life and a perfect expression of Spirit, I know that what is true of It is true of me, especially the power of my word to create my reality. Like God's, my word is Law in the Universe, and I speak it now.

Declaration/Realization:

I know, declare and affirm that the infinite, limitless abundance and prosperity of the Universe is everywhere and equally present, and as such is available to me now. It holds nothing back. The good of God is my good. Prosperity is my divine and natural birthright, since God always supports Its expression. God is within me, God surrounds me. It is above, below and all around me. Spirit supports, sustains, supplies, guides and guards me now and at all times, in every area and aspect of my life and in all situations and circumstances. All my needs are met, and abundant financial prosperity flows to me continuously now. There is nothing I need to look for or do, I need only recognize, open to, synchronize/align with and become an inlet for the infinite abundance and God-substance that has always existed and is all around me. I totally and completely release any negative ideas or false beliefs that once prevented my good from manifesting. There is no longer anything within me that blocks the abundant flow of my good. As I accept this truth, I attract and manifest now rich prosperity in the form of money, perfect health, loving relationships and fulfilling, creative self-expression!

Thanksgiving:

I am deeply thankful for this truth, for I know that my word is always heard and is even now a perfect idea in the Divine Mind of Cosmic Consciousness.

Release:

And so I release my word now into the Law of Mind, where it is set into motion now for immediate manifestation and for my highest and greatest good. I declare it done!

And so it is! Amen (optional).

This Treatment could be simpler or more elaborate, but it incorporates all 5 steps (including the 2 optional sub-steps of Denial and Re-affirmation) needed to be its most effective. Given with strong, positive feeling and belief (more on this further on) in its inevitable, perfect outcome, it is as sure and reliable a tool as any scientific law of physics.

## Treatment for Perfect Health

God is all there is. It is the Infinite Intelligence, Cosmic Consciousness and Divine Mind that is the creator and source of all that is. It is everywhere and equally present, filling all space, and It lives, moves and has Its being in, through and as Its creation. All creation, all Life is made of and created out of God-substance and it is perfect, whole and complete. In and as all Its expressions, God out-pictures as infinite, endless, vibrant energy, perfect process and circulation, functioning perfectly in, through and as all Its manifestations.

Recognizing this truth, I therefore recognize myself as part of and one with Spirit, a perfect expression of It. It is my source and I am created from It, as It. There is no separation. What is true of It is true of me, especially the power of my beliefs, thoughts and words to create my reality. Like God's, my word is powerful and creative. It is law in the Universe.

And so I speak my word now. I know, declare and affirm that as God in perfect expression, I am patterned after a divine idea and perfect blueprint in the Mind of Spirit, and I recognize that at my spiritual core I am whole, perfect and complete. Accepting this truth for myself, perfect health and wholeness manifest and out-picture in, through and as me. Every vibration, wave, atom, molecule, cell, fiber, tissue and organ of my being is saturated and immersed in the healing, perfecting and whole-ing energy and power of Spirit. Every part of my body works together in perfect oneness in harmony and order. It functions at 100% peak performance, assimilating, circulating and eliminating in perfect cycling. God knows nothing of imperfection or dis-ease, and so any condition within me which is unlike this divine perfect pattern does not belong, no longer has any power within or over me and is now completely and permanently released into the nothingness from which it came. I am perfect Life itself, radiating and expressing vibrant health, high energy, joy, wholeness and completeness.

I'm so thankful, knowing that my word is the word of the Divine expressing through me and is the truth as I know it to be. It is powerful and creative; it is Law in the Universe!

And so I release my word into the Law, where it is imprinted on Subjective Mind and is now in process for immediate manifestation. I am perfect health and perfect body now! I declare it done!

And so it is!

## Treatment for Love/Relationships

There is only God, the one Cosmic Consciousness and Infinite Intelligence that is the Creator and Source of all Life. Everywhere and equally present, It is perfect, whole and complete. It lives, moves and has Its being in, through and as all Creation. Once having created, Spirit allows Its creation complete freedom and total allowing-to-be, which is unconditional acceptance and love. Being the totality and all-ness of love, God expresses it through Its infinite creation and individualized manifestations.

Recognizing this truth, I therefore realize that Spirit and I are one, for I, like all of Creation, am a perfect expression of It. It is my source and what is true of It is true of me. Like God's, my beliefs, thoughts and words are powerful and creative, they are Law in the Universe, and they create my experience.

And so I speak my word now, knowing it is the word of the Divine. I know, declare and affirm that as a perfect expression of the Absolute, the unconditional love of Spirit is who and what I am, expressing, demonstrating and out-picturing in me, through me and as me. God-Love is within as well as all around me, and it supports, sustains, fulfills and maintains me. I allow it to radiate out and inform everything I do, and envelope everyone I come into contact with. As I love and accept myself exactly the way I am, a magnificent, perfect creation of Spirit, God's living enterprise, I find it easy, logical and natural to do so with others, for I see them as beautiful, whole and perfect out-picturings and expressions of the Divine. From this consciousness I attract people of like mind, spirit and heart with whom to share and for whom to care, for we are all one, created from, born into and immersed in and as omnipresent God-substance. Wonderful loving, fulfilling new relationships and friendships manifest for me now! There is nothing within me that can reject, refute or deny this God-love, which is who and what I am. By my very existence, I recognize that I am unconditionally loved, accepted and allowed-to-be by That which created me - it is a given! Being loved and loving, living in, part of and one with a supporting, sustaining Universe, I am whole, perfect and complete.

I'm so thankful for this truth! Immersed in, enveloped and warmed by the love of God, I know that my word is now a perfect idea in Divine Mind. My good is here now, and for this I am sincerely grateful.

And so I release my word, which is powerful and creative, into Law now, where it is imprinted upon Subjective Mind and does its good work, immediately manifesting in my experience for my highest and best good. I declare it done!

And so it is!

## Treatment for Perfect Work/Employment/Creative Self-Expression

God is all there is. It is the Infinite Intelligence, Cosmic Consciousness and Divine Mind that is the creator and source of all existence. It is everywhere and equally present and It lives, moves and has Its being in, through and as Its creation. All creation, all Life is made of and created out of God-substance and it is perfect, whole and complete. Within the allness of the Absolute exists infinite potential, possibility, variety, expression, freedom, ability and creativity.

Recognizing this truth, I therefore recognize myself as part of and one with Infinite Spirit, a perfect expression of It. It is my source and I am created from It, as It. We are one and there is no separation. What is true of God is true of me, especially the power of my beliefs, thoughts and words to create my reality. Like God's, my word is powerful and creative. It is law in the Universe.

And so I express my word now. I know, affirm and declare that I am a child of the Universe, from which I was born, live in and am one with. It supports, sustains, supplies, maintains, protects, guards, and guides me at all times and in all ways, showing me what to do, how to do it and when in all areas, situations and circumstances of my life. A living, intelligent, spiritual system, the Universe is the allness of potential, possibility, creativity and infinite expression. I am a unique manifestation of It, God's living enterprise. The infinite creativity and divine impulse of Spirit flows to me and through me as talents, abilities and skills that I love and are uniquely mine. As God always supports Its expression, It does so by manifesting these talents and skills through the perfect occupation and work for me now. It is work I love and for which I am ideally suited, appreciated, acknowledged and abundantly compensated. I work with compatible, like-minded people who are also doing what they love, and everyone benefits. I reject any and all false, negative comments, opinions of others or race consciousness beliefs that seek to deny my ability to attract and do perfect work that I love and enjoy, despite outward conditions or appearances to the contrary. As a unique, one-of-a-kind, vibrant, out-picturing of Life, I am here to express God in the highest expression It can be as me. I am in sync and aligned with the Absolute, the infinite God-substance which is always and eternally everywhere present. It is within me, I am immersed in it, it surrounds me and I don't need to go looking for it or "get" it. I don't need to "do" anything but open to it. And so I declare myself now a willing, accepting, open channel and inlet to which and through which the infinite abundant good of God can flow. I release any and all blockages and allow the limitless activity, creativity, potential, possibility and expression of the Universe to flow to me, through me and as me, manifesting in my life now as perfect, fulfilling work, joyful creativity and limitless self-expression!

Thank you, God! I'm so grateful, knowing that my word is the word of the Divine expressing through me and is now a living idea in Divine Mind. It is powerful and creative; it is Law in the Universe!

And so with the faith and trust OF God, I now confidently release my word into the Law, where it is imprinted on Subjective Mind and is immediately manifested for my highest and greatest good! I declare it done!

And so it is!

## FEELING, FAITH AND BELIEF

Paramount in the giving or expression of any Affirmation, Affirmative Prayer or Spiritual Mind Treatment, is the feeling, faith and belief within and in back of it. These attributes might be called the silent $6^{th}$ step, although they permeate the entire treatment. They are just as, if not more important, for they affect the quality and results of your request. A strong feeling of belief, conviction or intention is the Power behind your prayer and is what propels it, so to speak, into the Law of Mind. Feeling, faith and belief, unrestrained by fear or doubt, are the means by which your prayer is solidified into physical manifestation.

> *"The thoughts we think send an electrical signal out into the [quantum] field. The feelings we generate magnetically draw events back to us."*
> Dr. Joe Dispenza
> Breaking the Habit of Being Yourself

> *"Thought creates form, but it is the feeling that gives vitality to thought."*
> Thomas Troward
> The Edinburgh and Dore Lectures on Mental Science

I used to have trouble with the concept of faith and belief, thinking of them as blind, on-your-knees assurances and promises to an entity out there somewhere that I unquestioningly believed, without any evidence or logic whatsoever, that what I was asking for would be granted. I have since come to know that faith is in fact a spiritual act, *a mental attitude and activity* that transforms and shapes God-Substance into form. As stated above, it triggers the ever-present quantum flow of potential and possibility into actual manifestation. Rather than having a faith IN God (which implies the existence of a separate entity "out there"), it is having the faith OF God (which implies an omnipresent Power that is also within you). It is a given; steadfast, everlasting, constant, confident, totally without fear or doubt. Be mindful, always, where you are praying *from* as this will affect the results of what you are praying *for*.

When you have the feeling, faith and belief, as well as the trust, OF God, there is absolutely no question about who you are, the power of your word, the working of the Law of Mind, and the inevitable and certain manifestation of your good!

*Jon William Lopez, LSP*

*Commanding God*

# Part Four

# The Commanding God or "Goddammit" Treatment

I use the term "commanding God" throughout this book for good reason. Although Affirmative Prayer and Spiritual Mind Treatment are a positive and more effective step up from traditional prayer, sometimes the use of stronger, more assertive language, accompanied by stronger feeling, intention and belief is appropriate, especially when dealing with what we perceive as "big," "heavy," "overpowering," or "difficult" issues. (God, of course, knows nothing of "big," "little," "heavy," or "light." These are human perceptions, judgments and evaluations). Knowing how to use Spiritual Law to "make up" God's Mind is one thing. "Commanding" God, or the Law of Mind in no uncertain terms can bump up the results significantly when your prayers or treatments just don't seem to be working, or the personal need, desire or urgency is great.

When I first became active in New Thought teaching, my spiritual mentor, the late Rev. Helen Street, who was the spiritual leader at the Glendale Church of Religious Science in Glendale, California, called this kind of prayer a "Goddammit Treatment." (I credit Rev. Helen with "sparking my spirit" to become a practitioner.)

*Commanding God*

Rev. Helen Street

There are two major elements to a Goddammit Treatment: heightened feeling, emotion, conviction (even anger), and emphatic, assertive, no-nonsense, commanding language!

The strong feeling is up to you. Here, however, are some examples of strong and assertive words and phrases you can use in the declaration/realization portion (where you state your desire) of your affirmations or treatments:

- I affirm, speak, state, know, declare, assert, demand, decree, claim, command, compel, make so, order, announce, pronounce, require.
- I manifest, create, attract now, without delay, immediately, clearly, in no uncertain terms, with no ifs-ands-or buts, with authority, certainty, confidence

- I am exactly, precisely, clearly guided to, attracted to, led, shown. It is revealed to me now.
- I am shown what to do, how to do it and when, in ways I can clearly see, know, understand and easily take action on.
- I know / I clearly know / I absolutely know / I know in no uncertain terms / I know now
- I assert / I precisely assert / I firmly assert / I absolutely assert / I strongly assert / I assert in no uncertain terms
- I demand / I strongly demand / I firmly demand / I demand in no uncertain terms / I now demand
- I command / I absolutely command / I strongly command / I command in no uncertain terms / I now command
- I declare / I definitely declare / I firmly declare / I strongly declare / I declare in no uncertain terms / I now declare / I declare now
- I decree / I decidedly decree / I absolutely decree / I firmly/strongly decree / I decree now / I decree in no uncertain terms / I decree with no ifs-ands-or buts
- With the power and authority of God Itself I know / speak / claim / announce / now attract / now manifest / declare / affirm / assert / make so / demand / direct / command, etc.
- Some examples of statements using some of these words and phrases are:
- I affirm, know, assert and declare that perfect health is mine now!
- I strongly, definitely declare and decree that this unwanted condition no longer has any presence in me, use for me, or power over me! I release it totally, completely and permanently!

- I now claim, attract and manifest in no uncertain terms the financial prosperity which is my divine and natural birthright!
- My word is Law in the Universe and I speak it now with power, conviction and authority!

You get the idea.

A great example of strong, assertive language use was when I was living in San Antonio, TX, and my partner and I went to our minister, Rev. Cindy Flor, for some spiritual counseling. My partner was frustrated at not being able to find work and I accompanied him for moral and spiritual support. After completing her counseling, Rev. Cindy gave her closing Spiritual Mind Treatment and proceeded to inform God in no uncertain terms that It was *"on notice"* to manifest my partner a job within two weeks! We both blinked in surprise at the boldness of her statement, yet she was simply "commanding God," or the Law of Mind, to do what it was designed to do – reflect back into form that which was impressed upon it, no ifs, ands or buts! (Actually, the job took four weeks to manifest, not two, but as mentioned previously, the Universe sometimes needs a little "time" to arrange things for us here on the physical plane.)

Following is the prosperity Treatment from earlier, only this time written with much more assertive language. Notice how the wording, which are in italics, has changed. Try reading it aloud, with strong conviction and feeling (let the words bring up the feeling and create the conviction).

## A COMMANDING GOD/GODDAMMIT TREATMENT FOR PROSPERITY

I *recognize, know and declare* that there is only one Power, one Presence and one Divine Loving Source in the universe, creator OF the universe. It is everywhere present and fills all space. It is Spirit, God, the Creator of all Life and the infinite, unlimited source and supplier of all prosperity, good and abundance. *Its Law of Mind always says YES, reflecting back into form whatever is thought into It.*

Recognizing and knowing myself *with absolute certainty* as a part of God's Life and a perfect expression of Spirit, I *assert* that what is true of It is true of me, especially the power of my word to create my reality. Like God's, my word is Law in the universe and I speak it *with authority* in *no uncertain terms* now!

As I know, declare *and decree* that the infinite abundance, prosperity and *opulence* of the universe is everywhere and available to me always, *I claim my rightful share now!* The good of God is my good, and since God always supports Its expression, I know, affirm, declare and *boldly decree* that prosperity is mine by divine natural birthright. *I deserve and accept my good!* God supports, sustains, supplies and guides me now and at all times, in every area and aspect of my life and in all situations and circumstances. *I command the Law of Mind to continuously magnetize to me more than enough financial prosperity to always meet my needs and allow me to live fully, joyfully, safely, comfortably, securely, prosperously, healthily and abundantly, wherever and however I choose!* Abundant financial prosperity flows to me continuously now. There is nothing I need to look for or do, I need only to recognize, open to, synchronize/align with and become an inlet for the infinite abundance and God-substance that has always existed, *fills all space* and is all around me. I *totally and completely* release any negative ideas or false beliefs that once prevented my good from manifesting. There is no longer anything within me that blocks the abundant flow of my good. I am a money magnet! Income opportunities are revealed to me in ways I can clearly see, know, understand and easily take action on, resulting in perfect outcome. I synchronize my consciousness with the everywhere-present, infinite substance of Spirit and allow the infinite possibility, potential of the Universe to manifest in my life as free-flowing abundance and financial prosperity! As I accept this truth, I manifest and attract to me immediate opulence in the form of money, perfect health, loving relationships and fulfilling, creative self-expression.

I am deeply thankful for this truth, for I know that my word is *powerful and is* always heard, now a perfect idea in the Divine Mind of Cosmic Consciousness.

With heartfelt gratitude, knowing that my good is already given, I release it now into the Law of Mind, where it *does its good work and* is immediately and perfectly manifested for my highest and greatest good.

I declare it done!

And so it is!

How did that feel? Much more powerful, I bet (and hopefully more satisfying). Given with firm, assertive emphasis, feeling and conviction, especially when spoken aloud, its effectiveness is assured.

In commanding God, strong, no-nonsense language, accompanied by the corresponding strong feeling or emotion, can also be appropriate in other situations, such as a "talk" I once had with Spirit. Several years ago, I had to take on the responsibility of caring for my ailing parents. My father was suffering from dementia and my mother, who had a heart condition, was physically exhausted and could no longer handle the situation. Being the only child, it fell upon me to step in and take charge of not only their care but also their affairs. Several decisions, ranging from financial, to health, to their living situation, would have to be made, and no one could make them for me. From the moment I got the call from my cousin advising me of their situation, my life changed. Needless to say, I didn't have a clue as to what to do or how to do it! Within the space of a week I had to leave my life and career in

Los Angeles and move to Puerto Rico, where I was born and raised, and where my parents still lived. It felt like I was stepping off a cliff. Every morning for the first week I would curl up into a fetal position in the corner of my room and quake with fear. Yet I knew I had to take hold of the reins, hit the ground running and do what had to be done. Not only did I need to become my parents' caregiver, I also had to take charge of their financial affairs and decide what was in their best interests regarding their future. Once I'd made the decision that moving them back to L.A. to live with me would be the best choice for all concerned, there were hundreds of details that needed to be taken care of, in addition to their daily care. It was overwhelming to say the least! Feeling helpless, I sat down one night soon after my arrival and had a stern (ok, angry) talk with God. Sitting out on the back patio, gazing up into the star-filled tropical night sky, I declared in no uncertain terms that if I was the one who had to take on this situation then Spirit would have to show me exactly what to do and how to do it, because I literally did not have a clue how to! This was the first time I can remember actually "commanding" God, and I must say it felt good! The sky did not fall and I was not struck by lightning. In my declaration there was no room whatsoever for any fear, guilt or doubt, and when I was finished I felt a deep sense of peace, calm, certainty and satisfaction, sure that I had been heard and my point had been made, in no uncertain terms!

Within days, the pieces began to fall into place, and to my amazement (not to mention relief and gratitude) I was literally shown, step by baby step, not only what I needed to do but how to do it, where to do it and when. From all sides, one thing at a time, who I needed to call, what I needed to arrange and where I needed to go to accomplish what I needed to do showed up in front of me. Two of my cousins in particular, a close friend of my parents (my spiritual "sister"), and the kind woman and her son who had helped my parents out with housekeeping and household jobs for years, stepped forward and proved to be immeasurably helpful and supportive. They have my eternal gratitude and will never fully know the difference they made in my life. They are angels on Earth and I could not have shouldered the task without them. They truly embodied God showing me the way!

*Commanding God*

# PART FIVE

## POST PRAYER – GODDAMMIT AND BEYOND

As powerful and effective as Affirmative Prayer and Spiritual Mind Treatment are, there may be times when even a "goddammit" treatment doesn't seem to go far enough. When you're confronted by a challenge or a situation that seems so dire or insurmountable that even strong emotion (and even stronger language) just doesn't make the mark, there is an additional process, immediately following prayer, that you can do. And it uses no words.

I have repeatedly mentioned the importance of having strong faith and belief when praying, for these attributes are what give power to your treatment and affect the quality of the results you demonstrate. What gives faith and belief *their* power, however, is how *real* and *convincing* what you're asking for seems to you. You must pray from the assumption and certainty that your wish is already fulfilled, a given. And this is where this other process comes in. Since putting it into use, it has changed, or rather *enhanced* the way I do treatment.

Neville Goddard

I first learned about this process from New Thought author and mystic Neville Goddard (1905-1972). He was a contemporary of Ernest Holmes, but apparently they never met. In his book *"The Power of Awareness"* first published in 1952 (revised and reprinted by DeVorss Publications in 1992 by Victoria Goddard). Neville (as he has come to be known) taught that a person's *imagination* was God Itself, and it literally created your reality.

Basically, it is using the power of your imagination (as briefly discussed above) and the resulting *feeling* to pump up the reality and therefore the power of your prayer, and how clearly you, and consequently, the Universe, perceive it. It is the sensation of how *real* what you're treating or praying for that strengthens your faith and belief and solidifies it in Divine Mind – and subsequently your mind - for the highest and best possible manifestation. (And by the way, this process can be used following *any* treatment or prayer, not just the "big" or "heavy" ones.)

The process is as follows: at the conclusion of an Affirmative Prayer or Spiritual Mind Treatment, while still in the glow or higher consciousness of the prayer, continue in a relaxed, peaceful and meditative state and vividly *visualize or imagine* in your mind that you are experiencing your demonstration *now*, that it's already happening and is a part of your life and experience in the present moment. For example, you're driving that new car now. You're living in the house of your dreams now. You have more than enough money to always meet your needs now. You are experiencing vibrant, perfect health now. You are in your perfect, loving relationship now. You are doing what you love and are being paid for it now, etc. Be there, in the scenario, not just watching it. See it. Hear it. Touch it, taste it and smell it. Move through it. Fully experience and embody it. What are the feelings that come up for you as you imagine that your demonstration is a reality, right now, your desire is fulfilled? Do you feel happy, excited, joyful? Prosperous, secure? Healed, relieved, unburdened, light, free, fulfilled, peaceful, grateful? Indulge yourself and allow these feelings to permeate you from head to toe, *immerse and engulf* yourself in the experience, like soaking in a luxurious, warm, healing spa bath! Feel these sensations tingle around, within and through you. When you feel fully satisfied, whole and complete with the experience, free of all doubts, judgments, or "yeah-buts," gently, trustingly and confidently release the experience, knowing that you have made a strong impression and statement of truth upon Subjective Mind, which will now immediately and purposefully go about the business of manifesting it for you. Knowing that the result is secured, the ways and means for its accomplishment are set in place and will be clearly revealed and/or carried out in divine right timing and order. Do not concern yourself with *how* this will happen – let go and let Spirit, in which all solution exists, do Its job for you.

By the way, you can also do this process by itself without needing to do an entire prayer. Sitting or lying down, go into a relaxed meditative, receptive state. Declare your intention or desire to yourself and then picture and experience it, as described above, as already fulfilled.

I first used this technique to great effect when I was in a situation of dire financial need. I had no idea what to physically do or where the funds I needed would come from. All resources for work or other means of income seemed unknown, used up or inaccessible. My partner and I were basically homeless, staying with friends of friends. Every night after treating for prosperity (often after a "goddammit" treatment) I would remain in a meditative state and visualize, as vividly as I could, having the money I needed, and more. I did not censor myself or allow my "logical" mind to get in the way. In my visualization, I imagined walking up to the ATM where I banked, and depositing either a check or cash for as much money as I wanted (where the money would come from was not my concern, I already had it in my hand), then watching as the machine processed the transaction and showed the balance on the screen. The ATM would then print out a receipt, which I would take in my hand, look at and vividly see my new, abundant bank balance. This would then create feelings of immense relief, peace of mind, lightness (like a burden being lifted), deep gratitude and thankfulness. Not to mention utter joy and a profound sense of liberation and freedom (like being released from prison). I would often find myself smiling during this process and feeling relaxed and at peace. When I felt complete, I would then release the experience into the Universe, knowing that it would do Its part.

And in not too short a time, It did! Ways and means to new and unexpected income, where there were (seemingly) none before, were revealed to me and manifested for me. Avenues and resources I thought had dried up suddenly re-opened and became accessible again.

Sometimes, after a particularly stressful, tiring or worrisome day, I wouldn't even pray or treat at all. I would go to bed at night and, as I moved towards sleep, indulge myself in imagining my perfect world where money was not a concern for me whatsoever. I would envision myself living in the house and location of my dreams, doing my art, relaxing, gazing out at the magnificent view, traveling, indulging in and experiencing all my interests, cultivating new ones, being of service in areas most fulfilling to me, being with the person I loved. In short, doing what I wanted to do, when I wanted to do it, and with whom.

The Universe is an infinitude of *unlimited* possibility, potential, ideas, solutions, choices and abundance in all things, all waiting to be manifested. When we recognize, remember and *know* that we are expressions of It and are always supported by It, maintaining a synchronicity and atunement with It, Its limitless resources are ours to the degree that we believe we can claim them.

## COMMANDING AND CONQUERING FEAR

At this point, it seems appropriate to talk about fear. This emotion can undermine and even cancel the effectiveness of even a Goddammit Treatment or a visualization (by the time you reach the point of doing a Goddammit Treatment, however, fear should have no dominion). When believed in falsely, however, and allowed to take over, fear is the most debilitating, damaging and limiting emotion we have to deal with. Most of the time what seems like fear is only False Evidence Appearing Real. It is an ancient, primal emotional response that is triggered when we think our survival is threatened or when we are faced with the unknown. When you allow yourself to come right smack up against it, however, meet it full face, then take that next step through it, you discover that it's not a real "thing" at all, but a mental and emotional construct. The seemingly solid barrier you thought you couldn't penetrate becomes a veil of the sheerest gossamer through which you can easily and effortlessly step through, causing it to dissolve into nothing. Once fear is dissolved, the way becomes clear to handle what seemed so insurmountable or threatening in the first place, and solutions and choices begin revealing themselves immediately (not to mention an immense feeling of relief that in itself is incredibly liberating).

A most vivid example of this was when I was tasked with having to read and perform children's storybook songs for the first time in front of a live audience at a "mother/baby" convention the year my spouse and I taught English in South Korea. (I'd been hired by a company that published English storybooks for children.) I hadn't even begun teaching classes yet and here I was about to be thrust out in front of groups of eagle-eyed mothers with small children who'd be watching (and judging) my every move. I'd practiced three story songs and their accompanying movements the entire week before, yet once on site, every time I opened my mouth to practice before the performance, I would literally choke up and gag on the lyrics. I was in a panic! Why was this happening? I tried walking briskly, breathing deeply, repeating a mantra to myself, silently saying affirmations of peace, relaxation and perfect outcome. Nothing worked. With half an hour before "show time," I was ready to fling myself over the convention center balcony, knowing I would bomb completely and humiliate not only myself but bring shame and embarrassment to the company I'd just been hired at.

Then something amazing happened. From seemingly out of nowhere, I suddenly discovered that if I projected my voice to the front of my mouth, rather than concentrate it in my throat as I'd been doing previously, all compulsion to gag disappeared. My throat would not close up and I could breathe easily. I didn't know whether I could pull this off during a performance, but it was worth a shot. I made my way back down to where the company booth was. There was a large group of mothers and children already gathered. The music began, and, heart thumping, I stepped out in front of them, a big fake grin on my face. I hoped they wouldn't see that I was sweating. I launched into my routine and the next thing I knew, all fear was gone – there was simply no room for it since all my attention was focused on the task at hand. To my amazement and delight (not to mention relief), as I looked at the rapt faces of the children and, yes, the smiling expressions of approval from the mothers, I actually started to loosen up, enjoy myself and have fun. I concentrated on those faces and allowed their approval and joy to become mine. Some of the children even began to mimic my moves and we exchanged happy energy.

This same thing happened when I was first rehearsing my opening routine for my story reading classes. The opening bit consisted of 10 minutes of nonstop to-the-beat singing, speaking and choreography which involved interacting with the children, showing flashcards and pronouncing letters. Watching the other teachers do it made it seem perfectly easy, simple and fun, but when I tried it the words seemed to back up in my throat and I would start to choke, especially when getting to the flashcards (why at this particular point I never did figure out). Once again I was convinced that during my first class I would toss my cookies in front of the mothers and kids, and my career as an English teacher in South Korea would be over before it began. (Our mind loves to take fear and blow it all out of proportion with the most dramatic and outrageous scenarios!) The first day of class arrived. I sat in the school restroom stall and tried to breathe deeply and affirm perfect outcome. The fear clung to me stubbornly. I did some tapping exercises and that seemed to help a little. Finally marching into the classroom, I sat on my tiny little child-sized chair in front of eight mothers and children, who sat cross-legged on the floor in front of me. They didn't look scary at all, and in fact seemed eager and excited. The mothers were smiling. I smiled back, said a cheerful "good morning!" and started the music cassette tape going. The next thing I knew, I was filled with delight as I performed the "good morning" song, along with its exaggerated movements and, watched my audience singing and moving along with me. They already knew this stuff! In addition to the kids, focusing on the mothers' smiling faces helped a great deal as well and fed my confidence. All fear dissolved. I was doing this, and omigod, it was fun! I got to the flashcards and breezed through them easily, smoothly and effortlessly. Those classes became my favorite ones to teach.

Launching yourself into a task that seems fearful is the best way to conquer and dissolve that fear finally and forever. Since this kind of fear is only "false evidence appearing real," it has no power in and of itself except that which you give it. Going smack up against a fearful situation is the best way to move through it and dissipate it. Once you have done so you realize you've survived and are capable of doing much more than you previously thought you could.

As a perfect expression of Spirit, you already come hard-wired with the inner abilities and aspects of God Itself. All you have to do is go within and tap into them, affirm that whatever answer or guidance you seek is revealed to you in no uncertain terms, in ways that you can clearly see, know, understand and take action on in divine right timing and order. Demand, declare, decree! The Law of Mind will not move until you move it!

## TREAT AND MOVE YOUR FEET

> *"The creative process brings the materials*
> *and conditions for the work to our hands;*
> *then we must make use of them*
> *with diligence and common sense—*
> *God will provide the food,*
> *but [It] will not cook the dinner."*
> Thomas Troward
> The Edinburgh and Dore Lectures on Mental Science

Great! So now you've treated. You've spoken your word, declared, affirmed, commanded, visualized, felt your desire and released it into Law where it is now in the process of manifesting. What's next? You *could* simply sit back, catch your breath and allow God to do Its thing for you, giving the Universe "time" to bring forth the results you've affirmed for. There's nothing wrong with that – after all, you've done your spiritual work with faith, feeling and belief, and now the seed you've planted must remain undisturbed and be allowed to germinate. All well and good. You may recall, however, that Spirit can only do *for* you what It can do *through* you. Which is what the term "treat and move your feet" refers to. It means that once you've prayed, treated and declared your word, it's time to take action! The perfect new job may be waiting for you, but it's up to you to look in the classifieds section of the newspaper or go online and peruse opportunities on job websites. You may not know exactly what direction to take at first, but Spirit does. Taking one first step, however tentative, in the direction of your goal, condition, situation, or thing you wish to create, causes an amazing thing to happen – the Universe responds by revealing the next step, and then the next. When seeking direction, I often make the assertive, commanding declaration (whether it be in a "goddammit" treatment or not): "God shows me what to do, how to do it, and when, in ways that I can clearly see, know, understand and easily take action on for perfect results, outcome and my highest and greatest good!"

## PACK THE FIRST BOX

How to actually go about and implement or accomplish a certain idea, plan, desire or intention, especially if it's a "big," "difficult," or seemingly "impossible" one, is a common concern people have. Most of us are familiar with the phrase "Let go and let God." Although it has become somewhat of a cliché, the amazing thing about this statement is that in "making up" God's Mind this is exactly what happens. Once we state or put forth an intention or challenge into the Universe, the Law of Mind takes charge. We need not be concerned about how it will be accomplished, but we must be mindful, aware and receptive when ideas, ways, means and opportunities present themselves (and they will). Just take the first step and the Law, which is mechanical yet intelligent, takes over – predictably taking our thought (which is now a cause) and turning it into form (the result, or effect). If we know that the result is already a done deal, then it logically follows that everything needed to manifest the result is also set in place. Spirit reveals each step to take and we find ourselves compelled and guided to take them, moving forward to the desired result.

Jacquaeline Hellman, LSP, a Science of Mind practitioner friend of mine in Albuquerque, New Mexico, gave me a perfect example of this spiritual principle, which she called "packing the first box." With her permission, I relate it here in her own words:

"Our family of four (plus two cats) had been living in a single-wide trailer (from the Year One) on private city land, which had originally been inherited following a loss of a business, bankruptcy and bail from the desert of California, after the earthquake, when Highway 10 fell. Our credit was still shaky, but we had hope due to the equity gained from the land and trailer. We had no other cash or savings, had very little income and were barely getting by. We were living by prayer, faith and fear. It was the fear that was in the way. We could see no way to turn the only asset we had into a better homestead under the circumstances.

"Finally, one day I just gave in and decided to do the 'move your feet' part of "treat [pray affirmatively] and move your feet.' I didn't know how it would come about, but I decided to bag the fear and start packing. I had had it! So I went to Costco and bought around 10 large plastic boxes. I came straight home and packed that first box, then fervently started packing everything in sight and did not stop till every box was full. I just kept going every day. I had no clue what would happen. About 10 days later we received an offer on our land and trailer. All I'd done was put a sign out front (we had already worked on the trailer, cleaned up the land, planted flowers and made a nice walkway to the door – there was a lot of elbow grease put in over a few years, which all happened in the mid-1990s).

"The original value of the land was around $25,000 (a sizeable city lot) and the trailer was around $1700 (that's right, one thousand, seven hundred). The [offer we got for the land] was for $56,000 and the trailer offer [was] for $8000. We had a very short time to move out and nowhere to go. Before we knew it some good friends offered us a place to stay in their guest room, our kids stayed with other friends and our cats stayed with still others. We were all over the place for about a month. As it turned out, we ended up getting a mortgage and bought the very first house we had looked at (after looking at many). To top it off, the new house was at the opposite end of the block from my sister's family."

Jacquaeline's story is a perfect example of taking the first step, or "packing the first box." When setting out with an intention, or faced with a seemingly impossible or insurmountable situation, you may have no idea what to do next, but Spirit does. Once a first step is taken, It will respond by revealing the next, and the next. That first bit of action, even if you don't have a clue as to how your goal or desire will be achieved, is enough to trigger Divine Mind into creating a chain reaction, like a row of falling dominoes or set of opening doors, clearing the way before you and creating and revealing a path that shows what other steps or actions need to be taken, often one increment at a time, towards achieving what you wish to manifest or accomplish. So don't concern yourself with the hows, the whens and the wheres, no matter how apparently "big" or "difficult" your desire, goal or challenge may be. God, being an infinite, one Totality, knows nothing of size, proportions, "big" or "little," "easy," "effort" or "difficult." Put forth your intention, firmly set your goal, "command" It in no uncertain terms if you need to, and take that first step towards the achievement of that desire. If you don't know what that first step ought to be, ask (demand or assert) that it be clearly revealed to you (that in itself is a step), then remain open and receptive to receive a response. Every question has inherently the answer within it. Watch as the stepping-stones appear on the path before you! Declare in no uncertain terms that *God shows me what to do, how to do it, and when, in ways that I can clearly see, know, understand and easily take action on for perfect results, perfect outcome and my highest and greatest good!*

## REMAIN STEADFAST

After treating, even after a "goddammit" treatment, it can be easy to get distracted from and stray from your intention. Over time, the intense feelings you had when first delivering your prayer can lessen and fade. Fear, doubt and uncertainty can creep in again and take over. All your work will be neutralized and you'll have to start the process again from the beginning.

To prevent this from happening, or at least lessen it, it is important to stay focused on your desire and intention. As soon as you feel fear, anxiety, doubt, uncertainty, and even "logic" begin to creep back into your consciousness, counteract them by re-affirming your resolve and re-stating and/or visualizing your purpose, intention or desire. Declare and affirm something like: *This fear/doubt/uncertainty/anxiety, etc. has no place within me or around me, and no power over me! It is not real and I do not accept it in my consciousness. It is not the truth. I release it completely from me now and expel it back into the nothingness from which it came. I focus only on the good (thing/situation/condition, etc.). I affirm, declare and know that it is mine, already a perfect, divine idea in the Mind of God, in process now for immediate manifestation in my experience!*

This need not be a difficult, forceful or effortful process, in fact it shouldn't be. Simply notice when your focus and resolve begin to waver or lessen, then easily and gently, with the quiet confidence, faith and trust OF Spirit (because Spirit is who and what you are), shift your consciousness back to your desired good. Turn away from outward appearances, conditions and opinions, to a higher idea. Hold your good firmly but gently in mind. Know that anything unlike it has no place within, around, or power over you. While job hunting on several internet job sites, despite the appearance that there seemed to be no jobs I was suitable for, I kept looking anyway, day after day, knowing that *my* perfect job was out there and on its way to revealing itself to me! I refused to give energy to the "fact" of what appeared to be a lack of work and focused instead, even stubbornly, on the truth that *my* perfect occupation was there for me. It was, and soon manifested in my reality in divine right timing and order!

When faced with what seemed like insurmountable challenges and with no clue as to how to resolve them, I learned that, through steadfast focus on my intention, (what appeared to be) miracles could – and did – happen literally overnight. On September 11, 2001, I was flying back to Puerto Rico after a whirlwind week-long trip to Los Angeles to purchase a new house for my parents, my partner and me to live in. Upon landing in San Juan we were informed that an attack had occurred on the mainland of the United States (no details were given) and a national emergency had been declared! All airports, including San Juan International, had been shut down. I immediately had visions of World War III breaking out and of being stuck indefinitely on the tiny island of Puerto Rico, which is a major strategic American military presence in the Caribbean. Still, despite the rigid air travel restrictions that were then imposed for several months following that horrendous and frightening attack, I surged ahead with final plans to fly my folks back home with me to Los Angeles. I resolved and affirmed that nothing would stand in the way of that happening. Then, in continuing deteriorating health, two weeks before we were all scheduled to fly back, my mother passed away. My parents' house had just been sold, with the new owners set to take possession, plane tickets had been purchased and a new home had been purchased in L.A. Given my father's own deteriorating condition, delaying our departure and staying with friends or relatives would be problematic and burdensome. So, despite this tragic and unforeseen event, I was determined that after eight long months of steadfast preparation, nothing would stand in the way of us leaving! Over the next two weeks everything fell into place and my father and I (along with my mother's ashes) were on that plane as scheduled. My steadfast focus and resolve, despite the outward appearances and challenging circumstances, created a new wave of causation that turned them around into perfect outcome. I would be remiss in not acknowledging the amazing assistance, support and love of my family, extended family and close friends (to whom this book is dedicated) who guided and helped me through this experience. I am clear in knowing that God/Spirit brought these souls together as a result of my intention and prayers. I am forever grateful to all of you!

*Commanding God*

# Part Six

# Further Techniques and Tools for "Using" God

Here are some other things you can do and tools you can use to supplement, enhance and accompany your Affirmation and Affirmative Prayer work.

- Prayer Groups

    Praying with a group pumps up the power of your prayer. Knowing it is heard, or spoken back to you by others also gives it objectivity and helps to remove any personal doubt you may carry about it, especially if it's something particularly "big," "heavy" or "difficult." There are various forms a prayer group can take. In one, the group assists one participant in creating an affirmation or declaration, which the participant then speaks aloud to the group. The group then responds by saying together, "[person's name], I see you, I hear you, I understand you and I support your intention(s) with love." This is done for every participant in the group. In another form, a participant states their intention or the final results desired, and the rest of the group each delivers a step of the prayer (if doing a spiritual mind treatment), going around if there are less than 5 in the group. The person hearing their desire as stated by others is more likely to accept and believe the truth of it, knowing that those who spoke it have no personal agenda, fears or doubts attached to it that can get in the way of its manifestation. Then, of course, there is the one-on-one method with 2 people, in which one asks for prayer and the other gives it, then vice versa. Licensed practitioners and ministers often have their own private prayer partners with whom they can turn to for support whenever the need arises, or on a regular ongoing basis.

- Create a Treasure Map/Vision Board

    Although pooh-poohed by some as being rather simplistic and cliché, this is an effective visual tool for giving your desire a physical presence and power in your consciousness, and imprinting it in Mind. Find pictures that symbolize or show what it is you would like to manifest (or find a picture or photograph of the exact thing) and create a collage. Pin or tape your images up in a pleasing pattern on a bulletin or foam core board and look at, contemplate it, meditate on it, focus on it every day. Replace or change out your pictures as your needs change, or you find ones that better fit your desire. You can also tape your pictures into manila folders, which display when you open them. (This is an easy, portable way to take your treasure map with you to look at whenever and wherever you are.) Use a different folder for each area you wish to manifest. A 3-ring binder is another method, which allows you to organize your pictures into categories such as Love, Relationship, Prosperity, Health, etc. Supplement your images with words or phrases that symbolize your desire, such as "money," "prosperity," "riches," "perfect health," "peace," "love," "romance," "friendship," "happiness," "joy," "work," "perfect job," etc. You can get them from magazines or type them out in large, attractive typefaces on your computer, then print and cut them out, placing them strategically around your picture arrangement. If you prefer to go the high-tech route, select words and images online (or scan your own into your computer), arrange them in an image software program such as Photoshop or Illustrator and burn them onto a CD, upload them to your smart-phone, tablet, or print them out. Do what's most interesting, fun and exciting for you, as this will engage your imagination and make your intention and desire (not to mention the feelings associated with it) that much more concrete and powerful to the Law of Attraction.

- Prepare a Physical Space

I recently heard about a woman who wanted a new TV. She cleared a space for it in her living room and cut out an advertisement picture of the exact make and model she wanted, which she then taped to the wall in the space she'd created. The universe abhors a vacuum and within a month she had her new TV. Making or clearing a space for the thing you desire is a great way for it to come into your life. It is taking that first step, packing the first box, which creates a state of "room" or receptivity in Mind and triggers the universe into filling the void and creating or revealing the rest of the way for your desire to manifest. If it's a new car you want, clean out the garage. Clean out your closet if it's a new wardrobe you'd like. If your desire is for something non-material such as peace of mind, well-being, or love, visualize clearing a space for them within you mentally, or find a physical space you can clear that symbolizes that particular condition or state-of- being. For example, creating a space in your home for meditation might symbolize peace of mind and well-being. Assigning or choosing a space for exercise, whether indoors or out, might symbolize health. A special box, envelope, or place in your wallet for incoming cash could symbolize prosperity (you might want to actually keep an unsigned check for a specific amount – something that's realistic and attainable by you – or a large denomination bill, in one of those places in order to attract more). Some time ago I wrote a check out to myself for the amount of money I wanted each month in my checking account. I dated it "Now," wrote "Monthly Bank Balance" in the memo area, and signed it "GOD." On the back I endorsed it with my name, followed by the letters "tyg," which stood for "thank you God." I put it in my wallet and basically forgot about it. I now receive more than the amount each month I originally made the check out for. (I've since written out a new check for an increased amount, which is now in my wallet.)

- Keep a Gratitude Journal

    This is one of the most effective, easy and satisfying spiritual practices you can do. The more gratitude you have and express, the more the Universe provides you with things to be grateful for! Every evening before going to bed, sit down and write out at least 3 things you have to be grateful for that day, no matter how trivial or insignificant they may seem, even if it's for the hot shower you just took or the quiet time you've set aside to do this. Start with 3 things and watch how quickly and easily the list grows. Writing down what you're grateful for helps center you, calm you down after a stressful day, helps you sleep, and puts things into perspective, showing that there's a lot more good in your life than you may have thought. An attitude of gratitude also shows your faith in the Universe to always meet your needs and keeps you open to receive more. Give thanks even for things or conditions you desire that haven't manifested yet, as this triggers the Law of Mind to get moving and bring them into your experience! In fact, express gratitude for *everything!* Even though you may not be grateful *for* a certain situation or condition, you can still be grateful *in it*.

- Keep a Results Journal

    Keeping a record of the results and demonstrations you get is a wonderful companion to your gratitude journal and a great way to remind yourself about your ability to "command" God. It reinforces your confidence, encourages you to keep going and keeps you motivated, knowing and trusting that the Law of Mind, Cause and Effect and Law of Attraction work when you work them. Date each entry and include photos or copies of checks, correspondence, etc. You will be amazed at how quickly your results accumulate. At the end of each entry you might add a statement of gratitude, acknowledging that once again the

Universe has heard and supplied you. (You can keep a separate gratitude journal, of course.)

- Keep a Goals, Desires and Intentions Journal

    Write down your desires, goals or intentions (always in the present tense) and also read or speak them aloud twice a day, in the morning or at night (or whenever is most convenient). I usually do my gratitude writing before I go to bed and my affirmations or intentions in the morning before beginning my day. In the morning, create your day by writing down your intentions for that day. Know and declare that whatever it is you wish or need to do is a done deal and is accomplished smoothly, perfectly and easily.

- Meditate

    Devote at least 15-20 minutes a day to quiet your mind and go within to your center. Meditate, affirm, pray (see below), chant, focus on breathing, visualize, etc. Do this in the morning after you get up and in the evening before bedtime if you can. This quiets and clears your mind, relaxes your body, relieves you of stress, and prepares you for what your day may bring with ease, peace of mind and confidence.

- Treat/Pray Affirmatively

    Treating/affirmative praying at least twice a day is also highly recommended, first thing in the morning and before you go to bed at night. Declare your good silently or out loud if you can (aloud is more effective - see more below) and *feel* as though your desire is already a reality. Treat as often as you feel the need, impulse or desire to, as this reinforces the power of your declaration in your consciousness and in the Law of Mind, not to mention eliminating any new fears or doubts and strengthening and reinforcing your own resolve and belief.

- Speak Your Word

    Speaking aloud is a particularly powerful way to strengthen and solidify whatever desire, condition, thing or situation you wish to manifest. Remember, your words have power and speaking them aloud in a positive, confident, assertive, even commanding manner, along with feeling and acting as if you already have what you desire, powerfully triggers the Law of Mind into creating what it is you're praying for. You need not speak loudly (unless you feel the need and are in a situation where you're able to do so). Speak only in positive, present- tense phrases, since the Law responds equally and mechanically to whatever is thought or spoken into It. It cannot differentiate between positive or negative, now or future, but takes everything that is thought or spoken into it literally. Avoid words and phrases such as "I want." "I will." "I need." etc. because Mind will receive such phrases and words and mechanically keep you stuck in the sates of "want." "will." and "need." Instead, use phrases like "I manifest now." "I have now." "I now attract." "I am now." etc.


- Along with treating, speak your gratitude aloud as well. After making your list in your journal, say it aloud with feeling and thankfulness. I often write and speak my gratitude list after my treatment work at night before going to bed. It puts me in a peaceful, calm, secure state of mind and helps me fall asleep.

*Jon William Lopez, LSP*

*Commanding God*

# PART SEVEN

# AFTERTHOUGHTS: THINGS TO KEEP IN CONSCIOUSNESS WHEN COMMANDING GOD

- Always focus on what you DO want, not on what you don't!

  Why? Because what you focus on increases! The Law of Mind knows only what you think into it and does not discriminate, judge or evaluate. So if you always give energy, attention and lip service to any lack, limitation, ill-health or negativity in your life, that's exactly what you'll continue to manifest. Turn it around and give that same energy, attention and lip service to the good, abundance, perfect health and prosperity that you DO want to manifest and which is always available in possibility and potential.

  As it says in Matthew 13:12:

  *For whosoever hath, to him shall be given, and he shall have more abundance; but whosoever hath not, from him shall be taken away even that he hath.*

  (An interesting aside: the number-one selling board game during the Depression in the 1930s was Monopoly. While people didn't have a lot of money to move around in real life, moving around the monopoly board and getting rich with play money gave them a sense, or consciousness, of wealth. To this day, more money is printed every day for Monopoly than for the U.S. Treasury!)

- Talk to God.

    Whenever you feel the need or desire, have a no-nonsense conversation with Spirit. Speak until you feel complete and know that you've been heard. Aloud is effective and powerful (you may wish to do this in private). Writing (in freehand) is also powerful. Like in a "goddammit" treatment, demand, command and decree your truth in no uncertain terms. Put God on notice! Remember, Infinite Creative Intelligence cannot be offended, it is the Law of Mind you are talking to, or into, which responds intelligently but mechanically to your words, and the belief and feeling in back of them.

- Give thanks, express gratitude.

    Know and believe that what you've declared, affirmed, demanded or commanded has become a perfect idea or spiritual blueprint in Subjective Mind and is in the process of manifesting now. Trigger your desire into form by releasing your word into the Law with the calm, confident, faith and trust *of* God, then relax and allow your good to manifest for you.

- Let the Law work.

    Let the Law work for you undisturbed by worry, doubt or impatience. On the physical plane it can take the Universe a little "time" to rearrange itself and manifest or attract your good. With your Spiritual Mind Treatment, Affirmative Prayer or Affirmation you have planted a spiritual seed – allow it to germinate and grow. Don't "dig it up" to see if it's growing. You'll abort the process and have to start over again. If you feel the need to re-state or reaffirm your desire, then begin anew and continue until you once again feel complete, confident, calm and at peace. Keep at it until you get results!

- Keep your options open!

    Although it's important to be as exact and precise about what it is you'd like to manifest, give the Universe "space" to manifest your desire in ways you didn't specifically ask for, think of or expect. Being infinite, the Universe has lots more potential, possibility, solutions and ways of fulfilling your request than you, at your finite level, might imagine. Remember, the Law of Mind reflects back exactly what is thought into it, so even though you are clear on your desire, don't limit or box yourself in (in fact, if you can, get rid of the. A powerful phrase to include in an affirmation or Treatment for something you desire is "this, or something better." This allows the Law of Mind leeway in manifesting something you never expected but which could be light years better than what you thought you wanted. I did this a few years ago while putting out for a new way of creating income. The last thing I ever imagined was that an opportunity to go live and teach English to children in South Korea would present itself. However, it did, I accepted, and although it didn't seem like "something better" at first, the experience turned out more positively than what I would have thought. I made several new friends, one of whom connected me with the publisher of my first book, *Perfect Praying: 5 Simple Steps That Make Prayers Work*. There are hidden gifts everywhere, in everything, often where you least expect to find them. The Universe is a limitless, infinite storehouse of ideas, possibilities, potential and solutions, just waiting for us to align with them and become open, receptive channels for free-flowing manifestation. Give God the "space" to "think outside the box" for you!

- Trust your gut.

    You may sometimes have difficulty making a decision or asking for something, feeling uncertain as to what the "right" choice might be or whether what you're asking for is the "correct" thing for your highest and best good. That disquiet in your abdomen may be trying to tell you something. Your gut feeling is Spirit talking to you, your inner voice or intuition. Learn to listen to and follow it. Your intuition is God's Mind expressing through, in and as you. More often than not it's a feeling rather than a thought or words. Heeding it is probably the second-best way to "use" God. When caught in a dilemma or period of indecision, go within and check out your feelings about the situation. Imagine what it would feel like making a particular decision, choice, or having what you've asked for? If you feel light, happy, at peace, confident, sure, excited, fulfilled, etc., then you know this is the correct decision to make, appropriate thing to ask for, or appropriate action to take. If, however, you feel tense, uptight, doubtful, upset, stressed, conflicted, "not right," or any other negative emotion, then recognize that this choice, action, or thing you're asking for is not the correct one, at least not at the moment. Discard it and move on, considering other options until you hit on one that feels right! Your intuition/inner voice provides you with knowledge, information, solutions, direction and guidance from sources other than your physical senses. It's your access, your direct channel to the unseen, the infinite, to God's Mind, from which all knowledge, possibilities, guidance, solutions, and direction exists. It is always at your disposal and you can call upon and use it at all times, anytime. It is important, however, to learn to distinguish your inner voice from idle mental chatter, or wishful, fearful or negative thinking. Although sometimes strong (as in giving you a warning of some kind), your intuition is never fearful, negative or deprecating. Unless giving you a warning, it feels peaceful, certain and right. The attributes of true inner guidance include:

- a "knowing"

- a strong thought or idea

- a feeling of rightness, completion, certainty, satisfaction, peace of mind

- a feeling of urgency or anxiety (in the case of warning), which might not make rational sense at the time.

You learn to recognize your inner guidance by acting on these subtle feelings, thoughts and ideas and observing the results. True inner guidance is always right. You'll know this not only from the results you get, you'll feel good too. Ask God for answers and be aware of the response, whether it be a thought, feeling, idea, or mental picture. If you feel confused or stuck, affirm and trust that Spirit always knows, and will reveal the solution in divine right timing and order. It will show you the way, what actions to take, as well as where, when and how to take them.

- Begin noticing how things and/or conditions similar to what you're treating for or focusing on show up around you.

   One of my desires was to own a certain make and model of car. I soon began seeing it everywhere. Did that mean that I was creating more of this car out of thin air (or God-substance)? Of course not. It did mean that because of my focus, I was now paying closer attention, expanding my awareness and noticing the presence of the cars that were already around me, which I hadn't noticed before. What I was focusing on seemed to increase.

- Stay positive.

   Don't destroy the consciousness you've created with your prayer. Any negative thinking or doubt will wipe out what you've put into motion and you will need to start over. Don't dig up the seed you've planted to see if it's growing. Look for and focus on the positive despite whatever the outward appearance might be.

- Keep treating until you get results.

   Although your declaration is already a perfect idea in Divine Mind, on the physical plane it may take some linear time for the Universe to arrange Itself and bring that idea into manifestation.

Continuing to treat keeps the process in motion. Keep treating as often as you feel the desire to, and until you get results!

- Don't worry about how what you've prayed for will manifest.

    The Universe takes care of that. Infinite Intelligence not only lets Divine Mind receive what is thought into It, It also enables and directs It to create precisely the perfect ways and means to manifest and out-picture the desire. So take the first step, pack that first box and watch how the way is revealed. Focus and concentrate on the end results and let the Universe take care of manifesting the ways and means.

- Let go and let God.

    An often repeated statement perhaps, but that's why it's true. Once you've declared your desire and have released it into the universe, for heaven's sake give it time to work! Although in Spirit there is no time, and your word is already a perfect idea or blueprint within the Divine Mind of Cosmic Consciousness, it takes "time" on the physical plane for the Universe to arrange itself for you so that your good can be manifested. Situations, circumstances, conditions, people, must all come together at precisely the right point before what you've declared can come forth. Be patient! After all, once you've planted a seed, you wouldn't dig it up again to see if it's growing, would you? That would interrupt the germination process and might even stop it. Let the process unfold in divine right timing and order. In the meantime, continue to affirm and pray with faith, confidence and trust until the results you desire take form.

- Surrender.

    An aspect of letting go and letting God is the process of *surrender*.

    Surrender in this context does not mean admitting defeat or 'giving up.' It means releasing "ego," getting out of your own way and giving yourself a break! It is letting go of efforting, straining, or trying to force things to happen and letting the Universe take charge fully and do Its job for you. With faith and trust, surrender and know with quiet, calm certainty that the Universe will "hear" and reflect back to you what you have thought into It, without you having to "do" anything. Once the solution manifests, it is then up to you to take appropriate action (which is almost always clear, easy and perfectly laid out).

Declare and meditate often on this affirmation:

*I completely and fully release this situation/condition into Divine Mind/Subjective Mind, where it is now in process for immediate manifestation in my experience, in ways that I can clearly see, know, understand and easily take action on for perfect outcome and my highest and best good.*

Once you've set a process in motion, surrender your ego and the need to control, and let God do Its job. Declare and meditate often on this affirmation:

*Everything I experience has already been created in Mind and put into place for my highest and best good.*

- Trust.

As a spiritual being having a human experience, learning to trust and have faith in the workings of the Universe can be a life-long and challenging journey. We must learn and eventually *know and embody* that the Universe always has our back, and will always reflect back to us in form what we think into It. In that respect, God never fails us. No matter what the apparent appearance, circumstance, situation or condition, God is always there. If one door closes, another will always open and new options, solutions, choices and paths will reveal themselves. The Universe on a quantum level is an infinitude of possibility and good and we can access it in the amount and to the degree that we believe we can.

When doing Affirmative Prayer, always declare – *this or*

*something better!* The more we manifest and take notice of the good that appears in our experience as a result of our spiritual work, the more this builds up our level of trust in a Universe that always says *yes!*

Dr. Rev. Chris Michaels writes:

*"The spiritual journey is all about learning to trust. We learn that even though life circumstances may change, the only lasting truth is that God is always there. The Universe never fails us! God did not abandon Its creation. It is an infinite, eternal supplier of all that is good. When one outlet for good closes, we may rest assured that another one will quickly open. Learning to trust the Universe can be one's greatest challenge as a spiritual being. Letting go of the ego's need to strategize and manipulate one's good is an everyday task. But the one who can trust the Universe can say 'I don't know how my good will come, or from what channel it may flow, but I know it must come.'"*

- No matter what, maintain an attitude of optimism, confidence, faith, trust and belief.

Wake up each morning with the optimistic, joyful knowing, faith and trust that your day is already whole, perfect and complete. Give thanks. Express gratitude. Affirm and declare that everything you need to do unfolds and is accomplished easily and smoothly, in divine perfect right timing and order and with perfect outcome. Take everything a step at a time without allowing fears or doubts about what "might" happen in the future get in the way. If such thoughts do momentarily come up, notice and immediately dismiss them, and refocus on the positive, polar opposite. Your mind is not pre-disposed to either positive or negative thinking either way. It certainly was not created for negativity. It is neutral and you are the source of what you think into it.

- The Bigger Picture.

    When faced with or in the middle of a difficult challenge or series of challenges, all of which seem to be happening at the same time, or if your demonstrations appear to be manifesting too slowly and you feel frustrated, don't let yourself despair or become bogged down. Besides (or along with) doing a Goddammit treatment, take a step or two back, "rise above" your challenge, condition, situation or circumstance and look at the bigger picture, despite present conditions or outward appearances. When looking at a situation from a higher, more objective, or spiritual perspective, you can more clearly see the truth, the good and divine *process* happening *within* the circumstance than when you are stuck in the middle of it and have difficulty seeing a way out. This higher perspective can be achieved through spiritual practice - going within, becoming quiet and re-centering with Spiritual Presence. Then look and make note of all the good in your life *now* and see how the Universe has in fact been working to bring about this good all along and at all times. Notice how a past negative, or series of negative or difficult challenges and situations have all led, step by step, to a positive result. See if you can visualize a divine pattern, web, or blueprint, where one thing led to and connected to the next, where everything that happened was necessary for the final good outcome.

    This was made beautifully clear to me in my own life. My partner and I had moved to a new city, practically broke. I was delinquent in my financial responsibilities, we had no permanent place to live and no work prospects. Outwardly, things looked grim. I felt helpless, with nowhere to turn and, seemingly, having no choices. As a licensed spiritual prayer practitioner, it didn't seem like I was doing a very good job of walking my talk. In the midst of my apparently no-way-out situation, the only thing I could think of to do at the time was treat for perfect outcome, and yes, a miracle! To surrender to Spirit's will, not mine. Doing so seemed useless, since I felt like instead of sitting around saying affirmations, I ought to be out there doing something! Treating and moving my feet, right? The negativity of my mental state, however, made it next to impossible to know *what* to do or how. Still, in the midst of my fear, doubt and uncertainty, I groped along, asking, demanding Spirit to show me what to do, how to do it, and when. "What to do" had to be shown to me in ways I could clearly see, know, understand and *easily* take action on! Not too much to ask, was it?

Well, step by seemingly slow step, paths began to be revealed to me and opportunities were presented, "shown" to me. Gradually, one door opening would lead to another, and that to another in logical, orderly fashion. Each new door that opened would not have manifested had the others before them not also appeared. In only a few months time, our situation turned around 180 degrees. As one opportunity led to another, my partner and I were guided to an awesome new spiritual center, a wonderful new place to live (where we didn't have to pay utilities!), work doing what we loved, and our needs and financial responsibilities were being met.

It seemed like a slow, arduous process, until I took that step back, rose above the situation, and looked at my life from a higher, spiritual vantage point. What I saw was that my treatments had been, and were, working all along. On the physical plane, however, it was taking the Universe some "time" to arrange, bring forth, solidify and manifest the circumstances I was treating for. The thought-seeds I'd planted, despite being perfect ideas in Spirit, needed time to grow, manifest and solidify on the physical plane. The Universe had to arrange Itself to create and bring into form what I was asking for. From my higher point of view, I could perceive the workings and movement (as if in a giant, universal clock) of this vast divine process, which was, always had been, and continued working perfectly on my behalf and for my highest good *as I so directed It, and to the degree I believed I could.*

So the next time it seems that your good isn't manifesting as quickly as you'd like it to, take a deep breath, step back and "up" and look at what's happening from that higher, spiritual perspective. From that more objective point of view you'll be able to observe that the Universe is in fact continuously and at all times conspiring to bring about your highest and greatest good!

*Commanding God*

# PART EIGHT

## CONCLUDING THOUGHTS
### (AND A FINAL "REVELATION")

You are a perfect expression of that Higher Power, Cosmic Consciousness and Infinite Intelligence that is the Creator and Source of the Universe and everything of and in It. Therefore, what is true of this everywhere-present God/Spirit is true of you, including and especially the power and ability to literally create your world as a result of your beliefs, thoughts, feelings, words, choices and actions. You are a co-creator with God - It expresses, lives, moves and has Its being in, through and as you. It *is* you individualized and in expression and action. As such, you are endowed with the ability to direct that aspect of God that is intelligent but mechanical and impersonal, the Law of Mind, which receives the impress of your thoughts and through Subjective Mind reflects them back to you as a physical manifestation, situation, solution, result, or condition. Since this aspect of Mind has no volition of its own, you, in effect, "make up Its mind for it," give it direction, *command* it. It moves when you move it. Being neutral, the Universe is naturally, and at all times "on your side" always saying *yes* to whatever you think into it, focus on, pay attention to and demand of It. Doing so with enlightened, mindful consciousness, positively and assertively, with strong confidence, faith, feeling, trust and belief will result in a life that is happy, joyful, fulfilling, creative, healthy, loving, abundant and prosperous.

I've outlined several ways, tools and techniques, spiritual and physical, that you can use to "command" God and "make up" Its Mind. The truth is (and here's the final "revelation"), all these tools, steps, affirmations, treatments ("goddammit" or otherwise), do not do anything *to God*, nor by using them do you *change* God or the Universe. In truth, you do not literally manifest anything either. All things, states, situations, qualities, attributes, conditions, choices and solutions *already exist* as constant, perpetual, infinite ideas, possibilities and potentialities within the infinitude of Universal Mind and the quantum all-ness of Its totality. In "commanding" or "making up" God's Mind, what you are really doing is commanding and making up *your own mind (as an extension and individualization of God's Mind)*, expanding and shifting *your* consciousness *(as an individualization of God's Consciousness)*. By doing this you are putting yourself in a receptive space so as to *allow and attract* whatever *already exists* in quantum Spirit-Mind, *to* take form, rather than *making* them take form. It is God that does the "making."

*Everything* you need or desire is available to you now on a quantum, potential level, ready and waiting to be identified and called forth via your intention, then through feeling attracted and/or manifested. Being conscious of and embodying this means you are "in sync" with the Universe.

One of the ways you know you're in sync with and attuned to the infinitude of the Universe is that you *feel* and experience it. A sense of joy, connection, fulfillment, satisfaction, certainty, confidence, wholeness and serenity fills you. You feel prosperous, alive and excited inside, as well as serene and at peace. As within, so without - you notice, see experience and embody the beauty, color, divine design, magnificence, splendor, wholeness, abundance and prosperity of Life and Creation all around you, everywhere you look. You perceive and feel your oneness with this Divine, exhilarating, creative Presence that is everywhere present and fills all space. With joy you are aware of who you really are, a perfect expression and individualization of God/Spirit Itself, and this informs and transforms every belief and thought you have, every word you speak, choice you make and action you take. Maintaining this feeling of oneness with Life, being in tune and in sync with Universal Infinitude, plus being an open, willing and accepting inlet for Its all-ness to flow to and through you, is enough to "command" Infinite Intelligence and "make up" Its Mind on an ongoing basis without having to always "do" anything. Things naturally go your way, come to you, and you appear to manifest effortlessly.

Another way to know if you're in the Divine flow is simply by looking at your life and noticing if it's going the way you want it to. Are you happy? Fulfilled? At peace? Prosperous? Healthy? Joyful? Are you loving and loved? Are you loving your work, or expressing your talent and creativity the way you want to? If any of these areas appear to be lacking, you can choose to take steps to transform them, first from within, then, as a result, without.

Whenever you're feeling out-of-sync with the Universe, following is a Treatment that can help you to get back into spiritual alignment, bring comfort, peace, or quiet mind chatter (the Monkey Mind) so that you can hear God speaking. Rather than focusing on any one issue or need, it focuses on re-aligning with the all-ness of Spirit, from which comes all possibility, potential and solution, no matter what the outward appearance, situation or condition may be.

*There is only God/Spirit. It is the Creator and Source of the Universe, all Life and Existence, and is everywhere and equally present in, through and as all Creation. It is all there is. It fills all space. This Infinite, One Universal Intelligence and Cosmic Consciousness is all potential, possibility, solution, perfect outcome, clarity, and choice. It is infinite abundance, peace, order, perfect health, prosperity, unconditional love, perfect creative self-expression. The manifest universe is God-Substance physically out-pictured as directed by Divine Thought; it is infinite and everywhere present, and all form comes from and is made of it.*

*This therefore includes me. I am perfect God-Substance in perfect form, born from it, immersed in it, as it is immersed in me and surrounded by it. Since Spirit expresses within and as Its Creation, I recognize that I am a perfect manifestation and expression of It. I live in Spirit, as It, and am It. Spirit and I are One, It is my Source, and what is true of It is true of me, especially the power of my consciousness – my beliefs, thoughts and words - to create my experience. My word is law in the Universe!*

*And so, recognizing this truth, I speak/express my word now. I know, declare and affirm that I am in tune and in sync with the Divine Infinitude of the Universe from which I was created, am one with, and within which exists everything and all that God is. As an open, willing inlet for this infinite good, I surrender, allow and accept the Allness of God-Substance to easily and effortlessly flow to me, through me, where it now manifests and out-pictures in my life and experience as [insert your declaration – perfect health, abundance, prosperity, love, happiness, joy, self-expression, etc.]. My consciousness is a perfect, open inlet and channel for my good to happen; I attract it easily and it manifests effortlessly. I am now and always in the Divine flow. The ways and means for my good to manifest are already in motion and where appropriate I am shown what to do, how to do it, and when, in ways that I can clearly see, know, understand and easily take action on for my highest and greatest good and perfect outcome.*

*I'm so grateful for this truth and give thanks, knowing that my word is so for me as I know and declare it to be.*

*With the faith, belief and trust OF God, I release my word now into the Law of Mind, knowing it is powerful and creative. It goes forth and does its good work and is imprinted onto Subjective Mind where it is immediately manifested for my highest and greatest good.*

*I declare it done! And so it is!*

This kind of treatment focuses on shifting your overall *consciousness* so that you can become a clear channel and means by which your good *can* happen, flowing to you and manifesting for you, rather than "making" it happen. The term "healing is revealing," for example, means that all healing, physical or otherwise, is a process of clearing away inner obstructions, ideas of limitation, or blockages, like clouds concealing the sun, which has always been there. These blockages can be physical conditions or diseases, old false beliefs, issues, anger, fears, resentments, doubts, insecurities, etc. Clearing, dissolving, releasing and thus *healing* them *reveals* the spiritual wholeness, good, perfection and solution that *already exists as you* and was there all the time. Your "clear consciousness" now allows your good to reveal itself and flow forth to you easily, smoothly and effortlessly.

Stripped of all the bells and whistles, "commanding God" and "making up" Its Mind really is, simply, just a matter of your conscious awareness and knowing that Mind always responds to and reflects back what you think into It. I'd been reading and hearing this, in one form or another, since first becoming a student of New Thought teachings, but it was a while before I actually "got" that simple, yet so profound truth on a personal level. When I did, like the opening statement by Thomas Troward at the beginning of this book, it hit me like a smack upside the head. This revelation opened my eyes and filled my mind and soul, becoming part of every particle of my being. What triggered it for me was finding myself in the situation described earlier where there seemed to be nowhere else to turn and the only route left to take was to tell the Law of Mind what to do, "make up" (direct) Its Mind, and then surrender totally to It. I threw my arms wide, and, despite my fears, doubts, uncertainty, situation and all other outward appearances, declared myself an open, willing channel and conduit for the universal quantum infinitude of possibility, potential, solution and choice to reveal and manifest itself for me however it would. Focusing steadfastly on this idea, my consciousness expanded and shifted, and seemingly, "miraculously," my situation changed. It truly was a demonstration in no uncertain terms of God showing me what to do, how to do it, and when, since I personally didn't have a clue.

This shift in my consciousness and perspective has forever changed the way I do Affirmative Prayer, or Spiritual Mind Treatment. Now, rather than praying *for* my good, I pray with a consciousness *from it,* knowing it's already there in God-Mind, everywhere present, in the infinite quantum field of potential; there, my desire is already fulfilled, and I allow myself to become the open channel and inlet through which it can manifest.

You are made of, come from, are part of, immersed in and one with God-Energy and Substance. You are patterned after a perfect divine blueprint in the Mind of God which continuously imprints itself onto and into the perfect God-Substance you are made of and renders you perfect, healthy, whole and complete at all times.

All Creation consists of this God Substance and within It exists infinite possibility, potentiality, abundance, solution and choice. As a fish in water, it is above you, below you and all around you. It surrounds you and is within you. It *is* you! Unlike a fish, however, you can become mindfully aware of the Substance you are immersed in and made of. The Law of Mind thinks into and uses Soul/God-Substance to create and manifest whatever form It is directed to. And you can do the directing.

*You make up Its Mind. You command It!*

Declare:

*MY WORD IS LAW IN THE UNIVERSE!*

*AND SO IT IS!*

*Jon William Lopez, LSP*

*Commanding God*

# A Brief History and Explanation of New Thought and the Science of Mind

Since this book was inspired as a result of what I've learned from the ideas and principles of New Thought spirituality, Thomas Troward, and the Science of Mind philosophy, a few words about the origins and core concepts of these teachings at this point are appropriate.

The New Thought movement had its roots in the early 19$^{th}$ century with American philosopher Phineas Parkhurst Quimby (1802-1866), who was also a hypnotist, inventor and healer. He believed that all physical illness was the result of false mental beliefs and that a change in those beliefs and a belief in, and focus on, God's wholeness and perfection could heal any illness. Using his methods, he healed many patients.

Among the movement's other early founders were Mary Baker Eddy (a patient of Quimby's and founder of Christian Science), Charles and Myrtle Fillmore (co-founders of the Unity Church), Malinda Cramer (a founder of the Church of Divine Science), Thomas Troward (called "the father of new thought"), and Emma Curtis Hopkins (called "the Teacher of Teachers"). One of Hopkins' students was Ernest Holmes, the founder of the Science of Mind philosophy. Holmes was also greatly influenced by the teachings of Troward and Ralph Waldo Emerson.

The 1890s and the first decades of the 20th century saw many New Thought books published that included topics like self-help, mental training, financial success, and physical health. New Thought authors such as Napoleon Hill and Thomas Troward were extremely popular. Troward published many books, his most well-known being *The*

*Edinburgh and Dore Lectures on Mental Science*, 1904. Napoleon Hill was the author of the prosperity bestseller *Think and Grow Rich*, published in 1937.

The core concepts of New Thought are:

- Spirit, God, Infinite Intelligence is all there is and is everywhere and equally present. Its substance fills all space.

- We are perfect expressions of Spirit. We are divine in nature. God/Spirit lives in, through and as all creation.

- Focused, positive thought, in oneness with Spirit, is a force for good.

- What we believe, think and say out-pictures as our physical reality and experience.

- All illness has a mental cause. Physical illness is an effect of a principle cause.

- Positive thinking heals.

The three major religious denominations within the New Thought movement are Religious Science, Unity Church and the Church of Divine Science. There are many other churches, schools and organizations within the New Thought movement. I am a student of and a licensed spiritual prayer practitioner in the teaching of Religious Science.

Religious Science, or Science of Mind (RS/SOM), was founded by American philosopher and spiritual teacher Ernest Holmes (1887-1960). *The Science of Mind* textbook was first published in 1926 and revised in 1938. Holmes was greatly influenced by Dr. Phineas Quimby, Emma Curtis Hopkins, the writings of Ralph Waldo Emerson and Thomas Troward (whose opening quote at the beginning of Part One, was the inspiration and jumping off point for this book). Holmes learned about New Thought in Boston and later in Los Angeles. He did not originally intend for Religious Science to become a "church," but rather a non-denominational teaching institution. In 1927 he founded the Institute of Religious Science and Philosophy, although in 1949 the organization became the Church of Religious Science after several centers on Holmes teachings were established.

Like all New Thought philosophies, SOM teaches that God is all there is, living in, through and as all creation; all beings are part of and expressions of It, and we can therefore use Its power according to our degree of recognition of and belief in It. Since Spirit is not a "personality" but a "principle," Its Laws, especially the Law of Cause and Effect (every action has an equal re-action or result) and the Law of Attraction, work for and upon everyone with or without one's awareness. It can be positive, negative, creative, destructive, or neutral, according to the creative power of one's beliefs, thoughts, feelings and words. Through the use of Spiritual Mind Treatment, a 5 (or sometimes 7) step method of affirmative prayer used in SOM, people can proactively create and manifest what they desire in their life, or in the lives of others. Affirmative Prayer, or Treatment, differs from traditional prayer in that it does not ask or supplicate an outside, separate, removed entity/deity for favors or special consideration; rather, it declares and affirms the desired result knowing that it already exists as a perfect idea, possibility and potential in Divine Mind, the quantum sub-atomic field, recognizing a union with the Cosmic Creative Consciousness that is already within us (and all Creation) to achieve perfect outcome.

Before 2011, Religious Science consisted of two separate organizations (they had split in the 1950s mainly due to administrative, rather than spiritual differences) – the United Church of Religious Science and Religious Science International. They have since joined again to become the Centers for Spiritual Living (CSL).

New Thought is not a closed movement and continues to evolve over the years. Ernest Holmes himself considered the Science of Mind teaching to be "open at the top."

Thomas Toward wrote: "New Thought, then, is not the name of a particular sect, but is the essential factor by which our own future development is to be carried on; and its essence consists in seeing the relation of things in a New Order."

"The Edinburgh and Dore Lectures on Mental Science" Pg. 136

*Commanding God*

# ABOUT THE AUTHOR

Jon William Lopez is a licensed spiritual prayer practitioner with over a decade of experience in giving Spiritual Mind Treatment. He is a 30-plus-year student of New Thought philosophy, particularly the teachings of Thomas Troward, Neville Goddard and Dr. Ernest Holmes, founder of the Science of Mind. Lopez is a cartoonist, digital artist, photographer, author, teacher and former Disney artist. He has served on the boards of several Centers for Spiritual Living and is currently an active Practitioner at the Sonoran Desert Center for Spiritual Living in Amado, AZ. Using the principles outlined in "Commanding God" he lives the life of his dreams with his spouse in Green Valley, AZ.

His first book, *Perfect Praying: 5 Simple Steps That Make Prayers Work*, co-authored with fellow Practitioner Beatrice Elliott, LSP, is available through Amazon, DeVorss Publishing and CCB Publishing, Canada. It can also be ordered directly from the author.

*Commanding God* is Lopez's second book and is based on his original workshop of the same name.

*Commanding God*

# Quotes and References
(Listed in the order they appear in the book)

Troward, Thomas. *The Edinburgh and Dore Lectures on Mental Science*, 1904, 1909; DeVorss & Company 1988. ISBN: 978-087516-614-8; Pg 52

Holmes, Ernest. *The Science of Mind, A Philosophy, A Faith, A Way of Life,* R.M. McBride and Co., 1938; *The Definitive Edition,* Jeremy P. Tarcher/Putnam, G.P. Putnam's Sons 1997. ISBN: 0-87477-865-4; Pg 52

Chopra, Deepak. *The Seven Spiritual Laws of Success,* Amber-Allen and New World Library, 1994. ISBN: 1-878424-11-4; Pgs 71-72; Based on the book *Creating Affluence: Wealth Consciousness in the Field of All Possibilities,* 1993

Holmes, Ernest. *The Science of Mind, A Philosophy, A Faith, A Way of Life,* R.M. McBride and Co., 1938; *The Definitive Edition,* Jeremy P. Tarcher/Putnam, G.P. Putnam's Sons 1997. ISBN: 0-87477-865-4; Pg 70

Holmes, Ernest. *Living the Science of Mind,* 1984, Science of Mind Communications, De Vorss & Company; ISBN: 978-087516-627-8; Pg 308

Troward, Thomas. *The Edinburgh and Dore Lectures on Mental Science*, 1904, 1909; DeVorss & Company 1988. ISBN: 978-087516-614-8; Pg 51

McInnis, Noel. *Embodying God's Faith: The Company God Keeps and How to Keep It;* article, 2012. http://noelfrederickmcinnis.com/content/everything-site

Isaiah 45:11, The King James Bible, 1987

Dispenza, Joe. *Breaking the Habit of Being Yourself,* Hay House Inc., Carlsbad, CA, 2012; ISBN: 978-1-4019-3808-6 Trade Paper ISBN: 978-1-4019-3809-3; Pg 20

Troward, Thomas. *The Edinburgh and Dore Lectures on Mental Science*, 1904, 1909; DeVorss & Company 1988. ISBN: 978-087516-614-8; Pg 153

Troward, Thomas. *The Edinburgh and Dore Lectures on Mental Science*, 1904, 1909; DeVorss & Company 1988. ISBN: 978-087516-614-8; Pg 139

Flor, Cindy. Former spiritual leader of the San Antonio TX Center for Spiritual Living. http://cindyflor.com

Goddard, Neville. *The Power of Awareness,* De Vorss Publications, 1952, 1992. ISBN 13: 978-087516-655-1

Hellman, Jacquaeline. Licensed Spiritual Practitioner. https://www.facebook.com/jacquaeline.hellman

Michaels, Chris. www.chrismichaels.net

Troward, Thomas. *The Edinburgh and Dore Lectures on Mental Science*, 1904, 1909, (DeVorss & Company 1988); ISBN: 978-087516-614-8; Pg 52

Wikipedia, the Free Encyclodpedia. https://en.wikipedia.org/wiki/New_Thought

Troward, Thomas. *The Edinburgh and Dore Lectures on Mental Science*, 1904, 1909, (DeVorss & Company 1988); ISBN: 978-087516-614-8; Pg 136

# Image Credits

All images are either used with permission, are in the Public Domain, have been licensed for use, or are the author's own work.

Front Cover - "Modern Digital Thoughts," agsandrew, stock.adobe.com

Figure 1 - "Illusion of Mind," agsandrew, stock.adobe.com

Figure 2 - "Thomas Troward," portrait, Public Domain

Figure 3 - "Investigation on the Mind," Getty Images, iStock.com

Figure 4 - "The Tribunal of the King," Budapest, Hungary, James Finch, Pexels.com

Figure 5 - "Man in Black Jacket Standing on Rock Formation Under Starry Night," Christian Grigore, Pexels.com

Figure 6 - "Eye and Stars Design," iStock.com

Figure 7 - "Glow of the Mind," agsandrew, stock.adobe.com

Figure 8 - "Modern Digital Thoughts," agsandrew, stock.adobe.com

Figure 9 - "Person Holding String Lights," David Cassolato, Pexels.com

Figure 10 - "Universal Consciousness," agsandrew, stock.adobe.com

Figure 11 - "Reverend Helen Street," portrait, photo used with permission from Luann Paredes Ahumada

Figure 12 - "Silhouette of Man Standing on Mountain During Night," Stefan Stefancik, Pexels.com

Figure 12A - "Man Doing Praying Hands," shu lei, Pexels.com

Figure 13 - "Person Standing Under a Rock Formation On A Starry Night," Pixabay, Pexels.com

*Commanding God*

Figure 14 - "Neville Goddard," portrait, De Vorss Publications

Figure 15 - "Meditation," Activedia, Okan Caliskan, Pixabay.com

Figure 16 - "Sacred Site," Sedona, AZ, Jon William Lopez

Figure 17 - "Point Imperial Portal," Sabrina Caswell, http://www.sabrinacaswellphotography.com

Figure 18 - "Seven Sisters Constellation," Marco Milanesi, Pexels.com

Figure 19- "Jon William Lopez," portrait, by Gray Povlin

Back Cover Background Image - "Scenic View of Night Sky," Sam Willis, Pexels.com

www.ingramcontent.com/pod-product-compliance
Lightning Source LLC
Chambersburg PA
CBHW021012090426
42738CB00007B/760